THE MEASURE OF A
CHURCH

BY GENE A. GETZ

A Division of G/L Publications
Glendale, California, U.S.A.

Scripture quotations, unless otherwise noted,
are from *The New International Version*
© 1973 by New York Bible Society International.
Printed in the United States of America.
Published by the Zondervan Corporation.

Other Bible versions include:
King James Version (KJV)
Revised Standard Version (RSV)
© 1946 and 1952 by the Division of Christian Education
of the NCCC in the U.S.A., and used by permission.

Second Printing, 1976

Published by Regal Books Division, G/L Publications
Glendale, California 91209, U.S.A.

Library of Congress Catalog No. 75-17160
ISBN 0-8307-0398-5

CONTENTS

I would like to express special gratitude to my fellow believers at Fellowship Bible Church in Dallas, Texas who first listened to and interacted with this material. Their positive response was a continual source of inspiration to me to prepare this material for publication.

I would also like to express special appreciation to my good friend and colleague at Dallas Theological Seminary, Dr. Roy Zuck, who read this manuscript and offered several helpful suggestions. Roy and I have labored through various writing projects together and I am very grateful for his theological insights and literary skills.

WHY THIS BOOK?

What is a mature church? And how does it get that way? These two questions focus on what this book is all about.

Today there are a variety of opinions about the church—What it is! What it should be doing! When it's successful! Unfortunately, not all of the opinions—even among Christians in Bible-teaching churches—are valid!

There is only one source for finding the criteria for evaluating your church, my church, or any church. That source is the eternal Word of God. Unfortunately, when many churches that are often classified as successful churches are weighed in the balance of Scripture, and measured by biblical criteria, they are found woefully lacking.

To write a book of this nature is dangerous—especially when you're a pastor. First, it may appear that you think you have all the answers. Second it may appear that you are judging others. And third, you open up your own ministry to careful scrutiny and evaluation—and that can be threatening.

May I respond to these dangers by saying that if I think I have all the answers, I am terribly deluded. If I am judging others, I of all men stand in the need of being judged. And if I'm afraid to open up my own ministry to evaluation, I am then afraid to practice what I preach.

Several years ago, as a seminary professor, I began a new search of Scripture with a number of my students to discover what the New Testament church was actually like and why it was successful. What I and the others saw led us to the conclusion that what we are experiencing in the average twentieth-century church is not what God really has in mind. As a result of this experience with the Scriptures, I personally convenanted with the Lord that, with His help, I would do everything I could to help renew the church of Jesus Christ, to help it become what God intends it to be. And unexpectedly—which is not too surprising in retrospect—God led me out of the seminary classroom as a place of primary ministry and into a pastoral and church planting ministry.

This book has grown out of a personal concern regarding my own work for Jesus Christ in the local church. It has grown out of a deep concern that I personally might do God's work in God's way, that I might have a philosophy of the ministry that is truly biblical, and that I might have both proper goals at which to shoot, and proper criteria for evaluating my efforts.

Consequently, a series of messages I brought to my fellow believers at Fellowship Bible Church in Dallas, Texas, with the primary concern that *we*, as a body of believers, become what God wants us to be, developed into this book. My prayer is that you might join us in evaluating your life and the life of your church in the light of biblical standards of maturity. How does *your* church measure up?

Gene A. Getz

chapter 1

WHAT IS
A MATURE CHURCH?

Before looking at the biblical criteria for measuring the maturity level of a local church, let's look at some definitions.

WHAT IS A CHURCH?

The word "church" or "churches" (*ekklesia* in the Greek) appears 115 times in the New Testament. Three times it is used by New Testament writers to refer to a group or an assembly of people who are not even Christians (Acts 19:32,39,41). Two times it is used to refer to the children of Israel in an Old Testament setting (Acts 7:38; Heb. 2:12). The remaining 110 times the word *ekklesia* (or its plural form *ekklesiai*) is used to refer to a body of Christians—true believers in Jesus Christ. Thus in New Testament times the word "church" was not exclusively a Christian word. It was a word used by the secular community as well. However, it was given a new and special meaning when it was used by New Testament Christians.

When used by New Testament writers to refer to New Testament Christians, the word *ekklesia* was used in two ways. On several occasions, it was used to refer to the "universal" church—the total body of Christians wherever they might be. Primarily, however, the word was used to refer to a local church or a group of local churches—a particular group or groups of believers that were located in a particular community or section of the country.

Jesus Christ Himself set the stage for this double use of the word. He said: " . . . I will build my *church*" (Matt. 16:18, *KJV*). Later, when referring to a brother who would not listen or respond to correction from two or three witnesses, He said: "If he refuses to listen to them, tell it to the *church;* and if he refuses to listen even to the *church*, let him be to you as a Gentile and as a tax collector" (Matt. 18:17, *RSV*).

Obviously, Jesus was using the word "church" to refer, first, to the larger and total body of Christians He was going to call out to be His own people. He was not speaking of building a single church localized in a particular geographical area, but rather a single church that was made up of all believers everywhere.

But second, when Jesus said to tell it to the *church,* He was referring to a specific group of Christians located in a particular area—a group that could listen to a report and take action on that report. It is clear, from His directive and His expectation from those who were listening to that directive, that Jesus was referring to a local assembly of believers.

Again, when Paul wrote that Christ is head of the *church* and that Christ loved the *church* and gave Himself for her (Eph. 5:23,25, *KJV*), he was referring to the universal church. But when he wrote "to the *church* of God which is at Corinth" or when he referred to the doctrine which he taught "everywhere in every *church*," he was clearly referring to local groups of believers (1 Cor. 1:2; 4:17, *KJV*).

At times it is difficult to differentiate between the two uses of the word *ekklesia* in the New Testament. But for the most part it is quite clear that the word is used primarily to refer to a local assembly. This use of the word is far more prevalent in the New Testament. Alfred Kuen believes that out of the 115 times the word *ekklesia* is used in the New Testament, about 90 of them refer to the local churches.[1]

In the New Testament then, "the universal church was the universal fellowship of believers who met visibly in local assemblies,"[2] but these "local assemblies" were also called churches, even though they were visible manifestations of the one true church.

Also, it's important to note that the Bible never classifies a church as a "building." Thus today, the word "church" is not used correctly by most Christians. We often speak of the "church" that is "located at 4th and Main Street," whereas in the New Testament sense, the body of believers who assemble at 4th and Main are the church. But note! These believers are the church whether they are assembled or not. It is their position in Christ and their relationship to one another that make them a New Testament church.

But culture changes and so does language. In New Testament days they had no special buildings they called "churches." Rather, they met in houses, or earlier, in the Jewish temple and synagogues. But eventually, with the use of special buildings as a meeting place for the church,

14

it followed naturally that the building would also be called a "church." Though the word "church" was never applied to a building in the New Testament, it certainly is not wrong to call a building a church, as long as people realize that the church, in the New Testament sense, is really not the building but the people who use the building as a place to be edified and built up in Jesus Christ.

WHEN IS A "LOCAL CHURCH" A "CHURCH"?

It is easy to get bogged down with peripheral issues and questions. And there does not seem to be a clear-cut way to define a local church.

For example, is it when you have a constitution and regular meetings? Is it when you have baptized believers who partake regularly of the Lord's Supper? Is it when you have church officers, such as elders and deacons? Should numerous norms be present in order to have a local church? It certainly does not include a certain level of maturity; for the Corinthians were yet carnal but Paul called them a church. Further, it does not seem necessary to have spiritual leaders before you call a body of believers a church, for it is clearly implied that groups of believers throughout Lystra, Iconium and Antioch were called "churches" even before elders were appointed (Acts 14:21-23).

When, then, can a body of believers be called a church? I personally tend toward a simple definition: a body of believers can be called a church whenever that group meets together regularly for mutual edification. Jesus said, in the context of talking about church discipline, "For where two or three are gathered together in my name, there am I in the midst of them" (Matt. 18:20, *KJV*). And it is clear what Tertullian felt Jesus meant, for he said: "Where there are two or three people, even laymen, there is a church."[3]

WHEN IS A "LOCAL CHURCH" A "MATURE CHURCH"?

When talking about a "mature church," we can only really talk about *local* churches. True, the universal church is in the process of maturing and someday it will be totally mature—when we all are with Christ in heaven. But the only way we can measure a church is by what we can see, and, as will be shown, this is the only way New Testament believers could measure the maturity level of a body of believers in a particular location.

If a "church" is a body of believers that meets together regularly for mutual edification, how then can we determine when that body becomes mature? Or, more personally, what criteria can we use to measure *ourselves* to see if we have arrived at some degree of maturity?

Various Views of Maturity

Some say a mature church is an *active* church! They evaluate progress by the number of meetings held each week and by the number of different kinds of programs going on.

Some say a mature church is a *growing* church! As long as new people are coming and staying, they believe they are a maturing church. As long as the pastoral staff is enlarging, they believe "all is well."

Some say a mature church is a *giving* church! As long as people are contributing financially to the ongoing program of the church and supporting its many ventures, they believe it is a maturing church.

Some say a mature church is a *soul-winning* church! They say this is proof positive. When people are bringing others to Christ regularly, when we can account for regular professions of faith and regular baptisms, *then* for sure we have a New Testament church.

Some say a mature church is a *missionary-minded* church—a church that supports missions around the world, designating a large percentage of its overall budget to world evangelism.

Some say a mature church is a *smooth-running* church—a church whose organizational machinery is oiled with every degree of regularity. It is a finely tuned machine with job descriptions, eight-hour days, coffee breaks and punch cards. Everyone does what he was hired to do—on time and efficiently.

Still others say a mature church is a *"Spirit-filled"* church. This is the church that is enthusiastic and dynamic. It has lots of emotion and excitement. Everyone in it knows what his gifts are and uses them regularly.

And finally, some say the ultimate mark of maturity is the *big* church, with thousands coming to Sunday School and church every Sunday. Maturity, to them, is represented by a large paid staff, scores of buses that pick up children every week, multiple programs, a radio and television ministry, a Christian day school, a Christian college and seminary; and oh, yes, a printing press to prepare its own literature.

Unfortunately, some people really believe that what I have stated are actually biblical marks of maturity. And let me hurry to say that many of these things *will* be present in a mature church. There *will* be activity! Normally, the church *will* be growing numerically! People *will* be sharing their material possessions! People *will* be leading others to Jesus Christ and supporting missions! The church *will* be well organized! There *will* be a sense

17

of enthusiasm and excitement! And certainly there may be a number of ministries that develops out of a dynamic New Testament church!

But unfortunately, all of these things can be present without having a mature church. When measured by biblical criteria a church may be found seriously wanting in spite of all activity, busyness, and organizational structure.

A Biblical Standard for Maturity

The Bible is very clear regarding the criteria for measuring the maturity level of the local church. Paul summarized it in his letter to the Corinthians and illustrated it in several of his other letters.

PAUL'S LETTER TO THE CORINTHIANS

"And now these three remain: faith, hope and love. But the greatest of these is love" (1 Cor. 13:13).

Paul made it particularly clear in his New Testament correspondence what thrilled and encouraged him about certain churches. It was the manifestation of these three qualities and virtues—faith, hope and love—in each local body of believers.

PAUL'S LETTER TO THE EPHESIANS

"For this reason I, since I heard about your *faith* in the Lord Jesus and your *love* for all the saints, have never stopped giving thanks for you, remembering you in my prayers. . . . I pray also that the eyes of your heart may be enlightened in order that you may know the *hope* to which he has called you, the riches of his glorious inheritance in the saints . . . " (Eph. 1:15,16,18).

PAUL'S LETTER TO THE COLOSSIANS

"We always thank God, the Father of our Lord Jesus

Christ, when we pray for you, because we have heard of your *faith* in Christ Jesus and of the *love* you have for all the saints—the faith and love that spring from the *hope* stored up for you in heaven, and which you have already heard about in the word of truth, the gospel that has come to you. All over the world this gospel is producing fruit and growing . . . " (Col. 1:3-6).

PAUL'S LETTERS TO THE THESSALONIANS

"We always thank God for all of you, mentioning you in our prayers. We continually remember before our God and Father your work produced by *faith,* your labor prompted by *love,* and your endurance inspired by *hope* in our Lord Jesus Christ" (1 Thess. 1:2,3).

"We ought always to thank God for you, brothers, and rightly so, because your *faith* is growing more and more, and the *love* every one of you has for each other is increasing. Therefore, among God's churches we boast about your perseverance and faith in all the persecutions and trials you are enduring" (2 Thess. 1:3,4).

It is clear from Paul's letters to various New Testament churches that the thing that pleased him, the thing that he thanked God for again and again, was what he heard about the development of *faith, hope,* and *love*—but expecially *love*. In fact, as we've seen from Paul's second letter to the Thessalonians, he would actually hold up certain churches that had developed these marks of maturity as examples to other churches.

A Definition of Faith, Hope and Love

In future chapters we'll look carefully into what these marks of maturity really are—how they are expressed, how you can recognize them, and how you can develop them in the local church. But let's look at a brief and concise definition of each now, in order to have a basic framework of reference for our thinking.

Faith describes the confidence and trust that a local body of Christ has in its Head, Jesus Christ.

Hope describes doctrinal insight and stability, particularly in respect to our present and future relationship to God through Jesus Christ.

And *love*—a very profound concept in the New Testament—describes the relationships that should exist in a local church as well as the way that local group should relate to all men. In essence, love is the manifestation of Christ-like behavior by a functioning body of believers.

THE TWENTIETH-CENTURY CHURCH

If Paul sat down today to write a letter to the average church, to your church, how would he begin that letter? What would he thank God for? Would it be for the activities in the church? Would he refer to numerical growth? Would he begin the letter by thanking God for a large budget? For soul-winning efforts? For a finely tuned organization? Or a charismatic emphasis? Or huge edifices? *Or* would he thank God for the corporate *faith,* the corporate *hope,* and above all, the *love* for one another and all mankind that exists in the church? Would he actually be able to find many churches that measure up to this biblical criteria?

ACTION STEP

If you are a church leader, give your people an opportunity to respond to the message in this chapter by completing the following statements:

1. I thank God for my church because . . .
2. I believe my church could become more mature if . . .

NOTE: If you are not in a leadership role in your church, share this book with your pastor. Ask him to read it and give you his personal evaluation.

FAMILY OR GROUP PROJECT

As a family or group, complete the statements in the Action Step, and then share your responses with each other. Then spend time praying that God will help you contribute to the spiritual growth and maturity of your own local church. Brainstorm about what you can do as a family or group to reach this goal.

[1]Alfred Kuen, *I Will Build My Church.* Chicago: Moody Press, 1971, p. 51.
[2]Robert L. Saucy, *The Church in God's Program.* Chicago: Moody Press, 1972, p. 17.

[3]Kuen, *I Will Build My Church,* p. 51.

chapter 2

LOVE—
THE GREATEST
OF THESE

What is the greatest thing in all the world? Notice I did not say what does man *think* is the greatest thing in all the world? Rather, what *is* the greatest thing?

Obviously, many people think "status" and "power" and being a constant "success" are the greatest things in the world. That is why we've had so much emphasis on "competition at any cost"—which has led to unbelievable acts of unkindness and hatred toward others, often resulting in outright war!

Still others think "money" is the greatest thing! Some men will do almost anything to accumulate wealth regardless of the laws of society and the accepted principles of human decency. Many people lie, businessmen cheat, thieves steal, and prostitutes sell themselves—and all for one basic purpose—to acquire money.

But the Bible makes it clear that there is something far greater than status and power and wealth! It's *love!* This is the greatest thing in all the world—and always has been! And it's the most significant mark of maturity in a local body of Christians! Paul stated it clearly and succinctly when he wrote to the Corinthian Christians: "And now these three remain: faith, hope and love. *But the greatest of these is love*" (1 Cor. 13:13).

LOVE IS AN ETERNAL CONCEPT

Love is not just a New Testament concept. Rather, it is an eternal concept, related to the very essence of God Himself. When the apostle John looked for a phrase to describe God, he twice said, "God is love" (1 John 4:8,16). By this he did not mean that God is some immaterial force called "love," some eternal principle that is operating in our universe, as some have led us to believe. Rather, John meant that the essential nature of God, the living, personal God, is love. As He is "light" (1 John 1:5) and "spirit" (John 4:24), He is also love.

And how do we know this? Because "He sent his one and only Son into the world that we might live through him" (1 John 4:9). This, of course, was not just an act of love but the personification of love. God Himself became man that we might have eternal life (see 2 Cor. 5:18,19).

LOVE IS ALSO AN OLD TESTAMENT CONCEPT

On one occasion, an expert in the law of Moses tried to trap Jesus with a question: "Teacher, which is the greatest commandment in the Law?" Jesus' reply was jolting. He said: "Love the Lord your God with all your heart, with all your soul, and with all your mind. This," He said, "is the first and greatest commandment."

And then Jesus added a second: "Love your neighbor as yourself." For, said He, "All the law and the prophets hang on these two commandments" (Matt. 22:34-40).

23

Needless to say, the Pharisees were astounded. Furthermore, they were convicted, for Jesus zeroed in on one of their greatest weaknesses. He was telling them that they could not be good Jews unless they loved *both* God *and* their fellowmen, for you cannot have one love without the other. On top of *that* Jesus was emphasizing that burnt offerings and sacrifices were meaningless to God without love (see Mark 12:33).

Paul also confirmed this Old Testament emphasis on love, especially for one's fellowman, when he wrote to the Roman and Galatian Christians: "Let no debt remain outstanding, except the continuing debt to love one another, for he who loves his fellow man has fulfilled the law. The commandments, 'Do not commit adultery,' 'Do not murder,' 'Do not steal,' 'Do not covet,' and whatever other commandment there may be, are summed up in this one rule: 'Love your neighbor as yourself.' Love does no harm to its neighbor. Therefore, love is the fulfillment of the Law" (Rom. 13:8-10; see also Gal. 5:13,15).

LOVE IS ESPECIALLY A NEW TESTAMENT CONCEPT

A New Testament Directive

Though love is an eternal concept, and even though it formed the foundation for the system of law in the Old Testament, it did not reach its greatest expression until New Testament days. In fact, the directive to *love others* is one of the most repeated exhortations in the whole New Testament. It appears no less than fifty-five times—as a *direct command.* Note some of the following, which are representative of the total picture.

"Love your enemies and pray for those who persecute you" (Matt. 5:44). Christians are not only to love those

who love them, but also those who *hate them*. Jesus, of course, set the great example when, from the cross, He prayed for those who were mocking Him and physically abusing Him: "Father, forgive them, for they do not know what they are doing" (Luke 23:34).

"Love your neighbor as yourself" (Matt. 22:39). The directive to "love your neighbor as yourself" appears at least eight times in the New Testament, approximately half of the times in the Gospels, and half in the epistles. Our neighbors, of course, include not only our fellow Christians, but our unsaved friends and associates as well.

"Love one another" (John 13:34). The specific directive to "love one another" appears at least fifteen times in the New Testament—approximately five times in the Gospels and ten times in the epistles. It refers specifically to relationships within the body of Christ, relationships with other Christians.

"Follow the way of love" (1 Cor. 14:1). The way of love is a philosophy of life—a Christian philosophy of life. It gives a central focus to all that we do. It is living as Christ lived. The Corinthian Christians were following the way of selfishness and carnality. They were competing with each other and using their God-given abilities to put each other down and elevate themselves. Paul exhorted them to make their prime objective the "way of love"—not the "way of competition and selfish behavior."

"Do everything in love" (1 Cor. 16:14). *Everything* a Christian does is to be done in love. Paul admonished the Corinthians that even when they were taking a stand against false doctrine, they were to do it with an attitude of love. *Everything* is an all-inclusive word, but it is the Christian way. There are no exceptions. Anything that is not done in love is out of the will of God.

"Serve one another in love" (Gal. 5:13). A life of service is another hallmark of the Christian way of life. Again, Jesus set the supreme example when He said—"For even the Son of Man did not come to be served, but to serve, and to give his life a ransom for many" (Mark 10:45). Saint Francis of Assisi captured this thought beautifully in his simple prayer: "O Divine Master, grant that I may not so much seek to be consoled as to console, to be understood as to understand, to be loved as to love; for it is in giving that we receive, it is in pardoning that we are pardoned, and it is in dying that we are born to eternal life."

"Be patient, bearing with one another in love" (Eph. 4:2). Not all Christians are as easy to love as are others. But Paul makes it clear that we are to love them nevertheless. And this calls for humility, gentleness, and above all, patience and forbearance.

"Live a life of love, just as Christ loved us and gave himself up for us" (Eph. 5:2). Here Paul refers to the Christians' supreme example—Jesus Christ. Earlier, Paul mentioned the *way of love.* Here, he calls it a *life of love.* And this philosophy of life was exemplified by Christ when He laid down His life for us.

"Speak(ing) the truth in love" (Eph. 4:15). Even when Christians speak the truth, calling for correction in the lives of others, it is to be done in love. Paul made this very clear to Timothy when he gave him instructions regarding how to communicate to the people who were opposed to the truth: "And the Lord's servant must not quarrel; instead, he must be kind to everyone, able to teach, not resentful. Those who oppose him he must gently instruct, in the hope that God will give them a change of heart leading them to a knowledge of the truth, and that they will come to their senses and escape

from the trap of the devil, who has taken them captive to do his will" (2 Tim. 2:24-26).

"Husbands, love your wives, just as Christ loved the church and gave himself up for her" (Eph. 5:25). Paul lays a heavy one on Christian husbands. We are to love as Christ loved! This means loving our wives with the same humility, unselfishness and sacrificial attitude that brought Christ from heaven's glory to be born as a baby, to be laid in a lowly manger, to grow up in a home representing the lower class in His culture, and to deliberately die for the sins of the world (see Phil. 2:5-8). What a marvelous example for Christian husbands!

"Have(ing) the same love" [as Christ] (Phil. 2:2). Here Paul confirms what he said to Christian husbands in the Ephesian letter, but this time he applies the truth to every member of the body of Christ. We are *all* to have the same love as Christ.

"And over all these virtues, put on love" (Col. 3:14; also 1 Thess. 5:8). There is no greater virtue than love. Love, defined biblically, encompasses every virtue, as we shall see in the next chapter.

"Pursue . . . love" (2 Tim. 2:22). Love doesn't just happen! It must be pursued. It must be a goal for every group of Christians. There are things to flee and things to pursue in the Christian life—and love must be the highest goal!

"Let us consider how we may spur one another on toward love" (Heb. 10:24). There are ways to cause love to happen. As Christians, we must have in mind as our prime objective, especially when we meet together, activities that will motivate others to develop greater love. Thus, whether or not activities help develop love in a body of believers is an important criterion for evaluating what we do when we get together as Christians.

"Love the brotherhood of believers" (1 Pet. 2:17). Although Christians are to love all men, the Bible puts a strong emphasis on loving other Christians. They are to be given priority. (See Gal. 6:10.)

"Above all, love each other deeply, because love covers over a multitude of sins" (1 Pet. 4:8). There is *surface* love and there is *deep* love. Love should be an ever-growing and deepening experience within the body of Christ.

"Let us not love with words or tongue but with actions and in truth" (1 John 3:18). Surface love is *verbal* love. Deep love involves actions. It is one thing to say, "I love you"; it is another to actually love! Show it. The former is easy; the latter difficult. But love that includes action is *true* Christian love.

A New Testament Concern

We have many direct commands in the New Testament to love others. But further, a great concern of the first century Christian leaders was that love, in every body of Christians, *grow* and *mature*. As we've noted, Paul thanked God often for churches that manifested faith, hope and love. But notice the following concern expressed by both the apostle Paul and the apostle Peter:

In Paul's letter to the Philippians, "And this is my prayer: that your love may *abound more and more* in knowledge and depth of insight, so that you may be able to discern what is best and may be pure and blameless until the day of Christ, filled with the fruit of righteousness that comes through Jesus Christ—to the glory and praise of God" (Phil. 1:9-11).

In Paul's letter to the Colossians, "My purpose is that they may be encouraged in heart and *united in love,* so that they may have the full riches of complete understanding, in order that they may know the mystery of

God, namely, Christ, in whom are hidden all the treasures of wisdom and knowledge" (Col. 2:2,3).

In Paul's letter to the Thessalonians, "Now about brotherly love we do not need to write to you, for you yourselves have been taught by God to love each other. And in fact, you do love all the brothers throughout Macedonia. Yet we urge you, brothers, *to do so more and more*" (1 Thess. 4:9,10).

In Peter's letter to various churches, "Through him you believe in God, who raised him from the dead and glorified him, and so your faith and hope are in God. Now that you have purified yourselves by obeying the truth so that you have sincere love for your brothers, love *one another deeply with all your hearts*" (1 Pet. 1:21,22).

THE TWENTIETH-CENTURY CHURCH

If love is the greatest concept in the world (which it is), and *if* the development of love is to be the primary concern of a local body of believers (which it should be), then how does the average church measure up to this biblical emphasis? What is the primary concern of the average church?

Of course it is dangerous to generalize, but it seems that many churches are emphasizing good things, but not the *most important* thing.

For example, some churches give primary concern to how frequently and how well the Bible is taught. Now no one would deny the importance of good Bible teaching, nor the importance of it being regular and frequent. It is basic to Christian growth. But to observe the way some churches go about it, you'd think that they believe that Paul said, "And now these three remain: *faith, hope,* and *good Bible teaching*. But the greatest of these is *good Bible teaching.*"

Some churches seem to give primary concern to social relationships and fellowship. By their actions, you'd think that the Bible says: "And now these three remain: *faith, hope,* and *fellowship.* But the greatest of these is *fellowship.*" Again, no one would deny the importance of fellowship, but if it becomes the primary focus of the group, then they are departing from the New Testament emphasis.

Again, some churches seem to believe that Paul said: "And now these three remain: *faith, hope,* and *evangelism.* But the greatest of these is *evangelism.*" Well now, who could ever be against evangelism! Is it not one of the purposes of the church's existence in the world? It is! But there is, you see, something far more basic to New Testament church life. All these New Testament experiences—learning the Scripture, fellowship and Christian witness—are vital and necessary. However, these experiences should be directing us toward a goal—the goal of faith, hope and love. And that goal becomes the measuring rod to determine if we are having the right experiences and if those experiences are in proper balance. There is much evidence to show that a wrong emphasis will *not* lead to faith, hope and love—especially love. In fact, a wrong emphasis can lead to carnality, a problem in the Corinthian church.

ACTION STEP

How can *you* help your church to become a church that is growing in love? What are you doing to contribute to this process? Write out one thing you can do immediately and on a continuing basis to help your church, as a body, achieve this New Testament goal!

30

FAMILY OR GROUP PROJECT

Every Christian home or small group of Christians that meet regularly represent the church in miniature. Discuss with your family and/or small Bible study group how you can contribute to this goal of developing and manifesting love. If this is the most significant goal of the whole church, then it should be the most significant goal in our families and our small Bible study groups.

chapter 3

LOVE—
WHAT IT IS

The word "love" conjures up many different images and definitions in the minds of people. Some see it as emotion—a feeling, an attraction, or a passionate drive. Others, particularly those who are highly influenced by our twentieth century culture, see love primarily as sexual activity. This is very obvious from modern books, magazines and movies.

Though all of these things *could be* involved in the proper context of some expressions of love, the Bible presents a far broader perspective and a far deeper meaning than most of our contemporary approaches to the subject.

Biblical love is more than a feeling. Its most basic use in Scripture involves attitudes and actions. *And,* many times, biblical love must be expressed in spite of feelings. The greatest demonstration of this kind of love is seen in Christ's agony in the garden of Gethsemane when facing the reality of the cross. "Father," He prayed, speaking of the death He must die, "if you are willing, take this cup from me; yet not my will, but yours be done" (Luke 22:42). And in spite of incomparable feelings and emotions that precipitated perspiration that was "like drops of blood falling to the ground," in spite of His anguish of soul and desire to turn *from* the cross, He went on *to* the cross! And why did He do it? Because He *loved* us! You see, biblical love, Christlike love, acts and does the will of God regardless of feelings.

But how can we define biblical love? It is dangerous to oversimplify, but in a single word it is *Christlikeness.* Biblical love involves demonstrating those attitudes and actions toward others that Christ demonstrated when He came into the world and lived among men. This is why we are told on several occasions in Scripture to "love as Christ loved." (See Eph. 5:2; 5:25; Phil. 2:2.)

Note this—the majority of New Testament directives to "love others" were written to local bodies of believers—not to individual believers *per se.* This is very significant—significant because it is impossible for individual Christians living in isolation to carry out the *functions* of biblical love. It takes a body, a community of believers relating to each other, and encouraging each other, and building each other up to actually "love as Christ loved." (See Eph. 4:16.)

Not only can a "body of Christians" do *functionally* what individual Christians cannot, but also Christians, as a group, have *corporate* strength. And this we need.

We must remember that Jesus Christ was divine! Being God in the flesh, He *was* and *is* love! His capacity for unselfishness, humility, and self-sacrifice are limitless! Thus, when He went back to heaven, He left not just

isolated Christians to carry out His work but believers—
people who could express His love through local assemblies and groups. And the most exciting thing is that
if these local believers are open to doing the will of God,
they can be drawn together in a unique and seldom
known or experienced love relationship. Together they
can learn to "love as Christ loved."

Love cannot be easily defined, that is if we want the
total perspective. However, it can be *recognized!* When
it is present and growing it becomes obvious to both
Christians and non-Christians (John 13:35).

What, then, are its marks, its reflections? How can
we recognize love in any local body of Jesus Christ?
Fortunately, God has left us with some outstanding New
Testament examples, and we, through studying the New
Testament churches, can clearly recognize what these
reflections are.

THE CORINTHIANS

The Christians in Corinth are a classic illustration for
discovering both what love *is* and what it *isn't!* When
Paul wrote to four other New Testament churches—the
Ephesians, the Philippians, the Colossians, and the Thessalonians—he began his letters by thanking God for the
love that was being reflected in each church. But when
he wrote his first letter to the Corinthians, he departed
from his usual introduction and made no reference to
love. Rather, he thanked God for the *grace* that was
being manifested among them, for they were a very gifted
church (1:4-7). Paul even said, a few paragraphs later,
"I could not address you as spiritual but as worldly—mere
infants in Christ. I gave you milk, not solid food, for
you were not yet ready for it. Indeed, you are still not
ready. You are still worldly" (3:1-3).

34

Putting it another way, Paul was telling these believers that they were baby Christians when he was with them, and they still had not grown up. They were still an immature church, reflecting carnality and even acting like non-Christians.

Why didn't Paul begin the Corinthian letter by thanking God for their love? The answer is clear when you read the whole epistle. Putting it bluntly, they *didn't have any love!* Or if they did, it was so shallow that it was not recognizable.

And this brings us to what has often been classified as the "great love chapter" of the Bible—1 Corinthians 13. Unfortunately, we often read this chapter without considering the total context of the letter. When understood in context, we see that 1 Corinthians 13 is a rather unique condensation of nearly everything Paul had written to that point in the letter—a consistent reflection of their carnality.

First, Paul told the Corinthians (by inference) that *they had lots of gifts, but they didn't have love* (13:1-3).

Paul made his message clear even through his indirect approach. In summary, he told them that if he had the gifts of tongues, prophecy, wisdom, faith, and helps (as the Corinthians did), and yet did not have love (as they did not), he would be of no value to the Christian community or to the Lord. This, he implied, was their condition. Here they were, the most gifted church in the New Testament (that is why Paul thanked God for the grace given unto them), and yet they were an immature and carnal body of Christians.

Second, Paul told the Corinthians that *everything they did reflected carnality—not love.*

Granted, Paul's technique was indirect, but it was powerful! Rather than reviewing and cataloging their failures and reflections of carnality, he contrasted their weaknesses with reflections of love.

He told them that *love is patient* and *love is kind* (13:4). In other words, love is reflected by the opposite of what they were doing. They were impatient with each other and unkind in their attitudes toward each other. In fact, there were divisions and quarrels among them. Interestingly, this is where he began in the letter, describing their lack of patience and lack of kindness (1:10,11).

Paul also told them that *love does not envy, it does not boast,* and *it is not proud* (13:4). Again, the Corinthians were envious and proud. They *were* boasting (1:29; 3:21), and they were jealous of each other (3:3). They were not reflecting love, but carnality.

Paul told them that *love was not rude or self-seeking* (13:5). The Corinthians were putting each other down and using their gifts to glorify themselves. And when they observed the Lord's Supper, some thought only of themselves—they ate all the food and drank all the wine, purely to indulge in their own appetites while others went hungry (11:17-23). Clearly, they were not loving each other, but loving themselves.

Paul told them that *love is not easily angered, it keeps no record of wrongs* (13:5). These Christians were actually taking each other to court before non-Christian judges. Paul put it bluntly: "Is it possible," he asked, "that there is nobody among you who is wise enough to judge a dispute between believers? But instead, one brother goes to law against another—and this in front of unbelievers!" (6:5,6).

Again the picture is clear. The Corinthians were not a loving community but selfish and carnal.

Paul told them that *love does not delight in evil, but rejoices in the truth* (13:6). Not only were the Corinthians wronging and defrauding one another, but there was immorality in their church that did "not occur even among the pagans" (5:1). Get this! They were *proud* of it. They were delighting in it and rejoicing, rather than being "filled with grief" (5:2). Here was sexual activity totally outside the context of biblical love. It was purely selfish, sinful, and in violation of God's divine plan for sex within the sacred bonds of marriage.

Paul told them that *love always protects, always trusts, always hopes, always perseveres* (13:7).

Besides sexual immorality, many of these Christians were insensitive to weaker members of the body. They were not protecting each other, but rather, some were allowing their liberties and life-style to "become a stumbling block to the weak" (8:9). In fact, some were actually participating in idolatry (10:14).

Again Paul pulled no punches. When measured against the standards of love, the Corinthians fell short of the mark on every count. They were not bearing with one another. They were eager to believe falsehoods, even against their spiritual father, the apostle Paul (4:3-5; 9:1-3). They were also negative in their attitudes and constantly succumbing to the pressures of the world's value system.

Third, Paul implied that the Corinthians' *emphasis on spiritual gifts reflected immaturity, whereas an emphasis on love would reflect maturity* (13:8-13). And Paul made his reasoning very clear—gifts will pass away. They are temporary, but love will remain and continue. "And now," wrote Paul, "these three remain: faith, hope and love. But the greatest of these is love" (13:13).

THE EPHESIANS

The Corinthians are a negative example; the Ephesians

are a positive one. "For this reason," wrote Paul, "I, since I heard about your faith in the Lord Jesus and *your love for all the saints,* have never stopped giving thanks for you, remembering you in my prayers" (Eph. 1:15,16).

Paul, in his letter to these Christians, gives us another specific reflection of love. Exhorting them to "live a life worthy of their calling" they had received, Paul then wrote: "Be completely humble and gentle; be patient, bearing with one another in love. Make every effort to keep the unity of the Spirit through the bond of peace" (Eph. 4:1,2).

Unity is the hallmark of Christian love! It was a great concern of Christ before He went back to heaven. Thus He prayed for all of His disciples, and all of us, that we might be "one" just as He (Christ) was one with the Father: "I have given them the glory that you gave me, that they may be one as we are one: I in them and you in me. May they be brought to complete unity . . . " (John 17:22,23).

Where there is love—true biblical love—there will always be unity. This is why Paul reminded the Galatians that "the fruit of the Spirit is love, joy, peace, patience, kindness, goodness, faithfulness, gentleness and self-control" (Gal. 5:22). Here again, Paul was talking about the *functioning body,* not just individual Christians. Thus, he says, "Since we live by the Spirit, let us keep in step with the Spirit. Let us not become conceited, provoking and envying each other" (Gal. 5:25,26).

THE PHILIPPIANS

The Philippian Christians were, as a church, no doubt one of the most mature churches in the New Testament. Careful study will show that their activities and behavior reflected what the Bible defines as Christian love. They were a concerned and caring church. And even with a minor exception involving friction between two Christian women (Euodia and Syntyche, Phil. 4:2), they were a church reflecting unity and oneness of purpose. And they had no serious doctrinal problems, although Paul warned them against false teachers (3:2-4). And they certainly reflected a strong faith in God, which was clearly evident from their willingness to give, even out of their poverty (4:14-16).

But Paul was not satisfied with their present state. He acknowledged their love, but prayed that it might "abound more and more" (1:9). And then he spelled out how this could be done: "And this is my prayer: that your love may abound more and more in *knowledge* and *depth of insight*" (1:9).

And here we see an interesting correlation with Paul's concern for the Corinthians. Talking about the ultimate maturity of a church that we'll someday reach—when we are actually with Christ—he said: "Then I shall *know fully,* even as I am fully known" (1 Cor. 13:12). Here in the Corinthian letter, the phrase "know fully" is translated from the same basic word Paul used when writing to the Philippians. He was praying that they might abound more and more in *knowledge.* Thus, Paul's prayer for the Philippians was that their love might abound more and more in *full* knowledge—actually, *experiential* knowledge!

At this point we must ask, experiential knowledge of whom? The answer is clear from the whole of the New Testament. He is talking about an experiential knowledge of Jesus Christ and all that He is and represents. To abound in love means to come to know Christ better and deeper, and then to reflect His image to others. Thus

Paul wrote in the second letter to the Corinthians: "And we, who with unveiled faces all reflect the Lord's glory, are being transformed into his likeness with ever-increasing glory, which comes from the Lord, who is the Spirit" (2 Cor. 3:18).

And what will be the result of a full knowledge of Christ and depth of insight regarding His person? Paul spelled it out. The specific reflections of love in a growing and maturing body of believers are these. They will be able to "discern [that is, to distinguish, to come to know more and more] what is best." They will also "be pure and blameless until the day of Christ." And they will be "filled with the fruit of righteousness that comes through Jesus Christ" (Phil. 1:10,11).

THE TWENTIETH-CENTURY CHURCH

The supreme criterion for measuring the maturity level of a local body of believers at any point in Christian history is biblical love. Succinctly stated, love is a reflection of Jesus Christ. And to the degree a body of believers reflects Jesus Christ, to that degree they are manifesting Christian love.

But, some might say, this is a *generalization!* What is a reflection of Christlikeness? Let me summarize:

☐ Patience with one another reflects Christian love.

☐ Kindness toward one another reflects Christian love.

☐ Unselfishness toward others reflects Christian love.

☐ Humility toward others reflects Christian love.

☐ Forgiveness reflects Christian love.

☐ Honesty reflects Christian love.

☐ Christian morality reflects Christian love.

☐ Unity and peace reflect Christian love.

☐ A growing knowledge of Christ and depth of insight regarding the person of Christ reflect Christian love.

☐ Doing the will of God in all respects reflects Christian love.

☐ Being filled with the fruit of righteousness reflects Christian love.

ACTION STEP

Study carefully this list of traits that reflect Christ-likeness. Check those you feel could be developed more fully in your church and then write out one thing you can do personally to help the body of believers that you fellowship with to "abound more and more" in Christian love.

As you proceed, let me give you one word of caution from Jesus Christ Himself: "Do not judge, or you too will be judged. For in the same way you judge others, you will be judged, and with the measure you use, it will be measured to you. Why do you look at the speck of sawdust in your brother's eye and pay no attention to the plank in your own eye? . . . first take the plank out of your own eye, and then you will see clearly to remove the speck from your brother's eye" (Matt. 7:1-5).

FAMILY OR GROUP PROJECT

Using the above profile as a measuring rod for your family or group, evaluate your maturity level. Without judging others, discuss specific ways in which some of these manifestations of Christian love are being violated. Note: How you handle this project as a leader or how you relate to the group in going through this process will reflect how mature you are in your personal development. Can you participate "in love"?

chapter 4

LOVE—
AND THE
FUNCTIONING BODY

Biblical love is Christlike behavior. When it is present in a local body of believers it reflects maturity. But love also generates greater maturity, an even greater conformity to the image of Jesus Christ. A biblical definition of "love," then, embraces two interrelated ideas: what love is, and what love does.

"What love is" was the primary focus of our last chapter. Now we want to look at "what love does." Obviously, this second concept is an extension of the first. What love is and what love does are so closely related they cannot be clearly separated. But there is a distinction about what love does. I'm speaking of love and its relationship to the *functioning body*.

Paul expressed this idea well in his letter to the Ephesians. First, he emphasized that Christians are no longer to be infants, "tossed back and forth by the waves, and blown here and there by every wind of teaching and by the cunning and craftiness of men in their deceitful scheming." Rather, he said, by "speaking the truth in love, we will in all things grow up into him who is the Head, that is, Christ" (Eph. 4:14,15). We will grow up reflecting more and more of Christ's image. "From him the whole body, joined and held together by every supporting ligament, grows and builds itself up in love, as each part does its work" (Eph. 4:16).

Here Paul unfolds one of the most beautiful truths in the New Testament—the reality of the *functioning body!* Paul used a word picture. He used an allusion to the human body with all of its working parts. The Head is Christ. And the body is His church. The body is joined to the Head, thus getting its directives, its very life from Jesus Christ. But, said Paul, the body must function to grow! "Every supporting ligament" must be operative; "each part" must do "its work." Then, and then only, will the body build itself up in love.

We have then before us, a very significant question! What must a group of believers *be* and *do* to be built up in love? Obviously, they must first become a functioning body. But how does this process take place?

THROUGH CONVERSION

This is a rather obvious statement, at least to Christians in Bible believing and teaching churches. But it cannot be taken for granted. The true test of conversion is *love.* John left no question marks when he wrote: "We know that we have passed from death to life, because we love our brothers. Anyone who does not love remains in death" (1 John 3:14).

It's dangerous to become too introspective, but it's good to run a periodic check on ourselves. Are we loving

43

others? If not, John at least implies we'd better check our spiritual batteries! They may be dead! There may be no life in us. Maybe we just think we're Christians—because of our *"church*ianity." The true test is our personal relationship with Jesus Christ and to what extent we're reflecting His life and His love!

Now of course no local church exists that does not have some people attending regularly, or irregularly, who do not know Jesus Christ. In fact, that's good—if they are being exposed to the good news of salvation, and eventually respond in faith and receive Jesus Christ as personal Saviour. But it's bad—if they believe they are Christians when they are not! And it is doubly bad if they are hindering the body of Christ from being built up in love. And it's tragic, *very tragic,* when their spiritual leaders give them a false security, teaching them they are "Christians" because they've been baptized, they've joined the church, and they now support it regularly with their attendance and their material possessions.

Christian love, then, must begin in a body of people who have experienced true conversion. This kind of love can only be generated in the lives of true believers. It is in this context that the body of Christ can begin to function in love and unity.

THROUGH OBEDIENCE

Jesus once said: "A new commandment I give you: Love one another. As I have loved you, so you must love one another" (John 13:34).

This is a direct command! As Christians we have a choice. Either we love one another or we don't! Either we obey Christ or we don't!

This is really the essence of what Christ taught in His parable of the vine and the branches. If we remain in

Christ, we will *bear fruit*. And if we are growing as we should, there will be *more fruit*. And of course, the Lord's plan is that we bear *much fruit!* (John 15:2,5). And if you will look carefully at the context in which Jesus made these statements, you will see that the fruit He is speaking about is Christlike behavior, or more simply stated, *love!*

Many Christians take a very mystical approach to Jesus' teaching in John 15. Somehow they have concluded that "abiding in Christ" (see *KJV*) or "remaining in Christ" (see *NIV*) will create some kind of supernatural force that will suddenly cause them to be obedient to Christ. Obviously, the supernatural is involved, because becoming a Christian and living for Jesus Christ is a supernatural experience. But, here in this passage, Jesus was simply issuing a command. Further, He said, "If you obey my commands, you will remain in my love, just as I have obeyed my Father's commands and remain in his love" (John 15:10). And then, just to make sure His disciples understood, Jesus said again, "My command is this: Love each other as I have loved you" (John 15:12).

It is possible, then, for a group of Christians to disobey Christ when it comes to loving each other. Evidently this is what happened to the church at Ephesus over a period of time. Remember? When Paul first wrote to these Christians they were one of the most mature bodies of believers in the New Testament. Paul began his letter by thanking God for their faith and their *love* (Eph. 1:15). But then the apostle John wrote to them about thirty-five years later. As he wrote, he spoke on behalf of Jesus Christ and chided them for having *forsaken their first love* (Rev. 2:4). "Remember the height from which you have fallen! Repent and do the things you did at first" (Rev. 2:5).

Significantly, John began this little letter (Rev. 2:1-7) by commending them for their doctrinal purity and perseverance in standing against false teaching. But, is it possible to be doctrinally pure and yet to reflect little of Christ's love? Obviously, from the text of this Scripture, it is! Here were New Testament Christians who had allowed their Christian lives to deteriorate to a state of infancy. In fact, they had become so carnal that Christ gave them a stern warning: "If you do not repent [change], I will come to you and remove your lampstand from its place" (Rev. 2:5).

But don't miss the most important point! The body of believers at Ephesus was disobeying Christ. This second generation of Christians was not doing what He said. They had deliberately failed to carry out His command—to love others as they had done at first. They were not abiding or remaining in Him. To be a functioning body, building ourselves up in love, means we must be obedient to the commands of Christ.

THROUGH PARTICIPATION

What love *is* and how it can be recognized was described in the previous chapter. Patience, kindness, unselfishness, humility, forgiveness, honesty, morality, unity, insight, obedience and righteous living are all key words that are used to reflect the love that existed—or did not exist—in the churches at Corinth, Ephesus, and Philippi.

But let's take another step. Though closely related to what love *is,* let's look more specifically at what love *does,* and how the body functions and builds itself up as a result of love. The key word is *participation!*

The body will build "itself up in love, as each part does its work" (Eph. 4:16). There is no place for spectators in the body of Christ. Just as every part of the human body must operate properly for effective function, so every believer must do his part. Everyone is needed and is important.

The body will build itself up in love when there is "equal concern for each other" (1 Cor. 12:25). This was a distinct problem in Corinth. Some members of the body thought they were more important than others. They were putting each other down. Thus Paul wrote: "The eye cannot say to the hand, 'I don't need you!' And the head cannot say to the feet, 'I don't need you!' On the contrary," said Paul, "those parts of the body that seem to be weaker are indispensable" (1 Cor. 12:21,22). In other words, every member is needed and every member must function if the body of Christ is to continue to build itself up in love.

The body will build itself up in love when we "serve one another in love" (Gal. 5:13). A Christian life-style should pulsate with one major ingredient—"ask not what you can get, but what you can give." This is love in action! Think of what would happen in any local church if every Christian in the body functioned with this goal in mind!

The body will build itself up in love when we bear "with one another in love" (Eph. 4:2). Bearing with other members of the body of Christ means being patient and understanding. It means tolerating weaknesses and genuinely and graciously helping those who need to grow and mature in Christ. It does not, of course, mean tolerating flagrant and continual sin, but rather being an understanding and helping person. "Brothers," wrote Paul to the Galatians, "if a man is trapped in some sin, you who are spiritual should restore him gently" (Gal. 6:1).

The body will build itself up in love when we "carry each other's burdens" (Gal. 6:2). When one part of the

47

human body hurts, usually the whole body is affected. "If one part suffers, every part suffers with it," wrote Paul (1 Cor. 12:26).

So it should be with the body of Christ. We are to "rejoice with those who rejoice" and "mourn with those who mourn" (Rom. 12:15). And James adds: "Is any one of you sick? He should call the elders of the church to pray over him and anoint him with oil in the name of the Lord" (Jas. 5:14).

The body will build itself up in love when we "encourage one another and build each other up" (1 Thess. 5:11). Some Christians seem to have the "gift of discouragement." They seem to always have something negative to say about other Christians. And if they refrain from saying something negative, they don't say *anything,* which can be just as bad, or even worse.

It's amazing what Christians can do with words. It is possible to change a person's whole day by what one person says to another. Christians need regular encouragement. The author of the letter to the Hebrews knew the value of this concept and wrote: "Encourage one another daily" (Heb. 3:13).

The amazing thing is that words are so easy to use, and cost so little! And yet they pay rich dividends. In fact, the book of Proverbs tells us that pleasant words are like a "honeycomb, sweet to the soul, and health to the bones" (Prov. 16:24, *KJV*). And when they are chosen properly they are like "apples of gold in a setting of silver" (Prov. 25:11, *RSV*).

Paul was very much aware of the power of words. To the Ephesians he wrote: "Do not let any unwholesome talk come out of your mouths, but only what is helpful for building others up according to their needs, that it may benefit those who listen" (Eph. 4:29). And the author

48

of the book of Hebrews clearly states that one reason why the body of Christ should meet regularly is to, "Consider how we may spur one another on toward love and good deeds. Let us not give up meeting together, as some are in the habit of doing, but let us encourage one another—and all the more as you see the Day approaching" (Heb. 10:24,25).

The body will build itself up in love when we "submit to one another out of reverence for Christ" (Eph. 5:21). Submissiveness is the opposite of selfish and self-centered behavior. "Do nothing out of selfish ambition or vain conceit," wrote Paul to the Philippians, "but in humility consider others better than yourselves. Each of you should look not only to your own interests, but also to the interests of others" (Phil. 2:3,4).

Unfortunately, some Christians can never make way for someone else. If they are not the center of attention, they are unhappy and distraught. If they don't have the last word, they are frustrated. This, of course, is not the Christian way! It is certainly not the way of love!

The body will build itself up in love when we forgive one another (Eph. 4:32). At the heart of Christianity is the concept of forgiveness. This is why God sent Jesus Christ to die for the sins of the world. He made provision for the *forgiveness* of our sins. Thus Paul exhorted the Colossians—"forgive whatever grievances you may have against one another. Forgive as the Lord forgave you" (Col. 3:13).

How can he who has experienced the marvelous grace of God in forgiveness and salvation fail to forgive others? And yet there are Christians who for years carry deep grudges and bitterness toward other Christians. In some instances, unforgiveness is directed toward a husband or a wife, or a father or a mother, or a son or a daughter!

49

We cannot miss the message of the Scriptures. The "way of love" is the "way of forgiveness." One day Peter came to Jesus and asked, "Lord, how many times shall I forgive my brother when he sins against me? Up to seven times?"

Jesus' answer is staggering! "I tell you, not seven times, but seventy-seven times [or seventy times seven]" (Matt. 18:21,22).

The body will build itself up in love when we are honest with one another (Col. 3:9). One of the characteristics of the New Testament pagan community was dishonesty. And how reflective this is of our own twentieth-century culture! Who can be trusted? Lying and cheating permeate all levels of government, business, and social activities. Even the family structure has been deeply affected by dishonesty.

But Christians are to be different. To the Colossians, Paul wrote: "Do not lie to each other, since you have taken off your old self with its practices and have put on the new self, which is being renewed in knowledge in the image of its Creator" (Col. 3:9,10). And James added the same dimension to his epistle when he said: "Brothers, do not slander one another" (Jas. 4:11). And later he added: "Don't grumble against each other, brothers, or you will be judged" (Jas. 5:9). Again, the "way of love" is the "way of honesty."

The body will build itself up in love when we "offer hospitality to one another without grumbling" (1 Pet. 4:9). Hospitality means sharing what we have with others. Obviously, its expressions vary with cultural situations. But it is a biblical command and a mark of Christian maturity. Thus Paul wrote that a man who desires a spiritual leadership role in the church must be "hospitable"

(1 Tim. 3:2; Titus 1:8). But this quality of life is to be practiced by all members of Christ's body—not just elders.

Let me hasten to add that the Bible is a marvelous book of balances. While it commands us to be hospitable, it also condemns those who take advantage of other peoples's love and graciousness. Evidently some Christians in the Thessalonian church were doing this very thing and Paul dealt with it in no uncertain terms: "If a man will not work, he shall not eat" (2 Thess. 3:10).

The body will build itself up when we "teach and counsel one another with all wisdom" (Col. 3:16). Some people believe that the responsibility for teaching and counseling members of the body of Christ belongs to the pastor or the elders.[1] And this, of course, is partially true. But the Bible teaches that *every* member of the body of Christ is to be involved in this process (Eph. 5:19).

But notice that we are to teach and counsel one another with "all wisdom." This Pauline directive does not give the Christian license to attack other Christians; to look for other people's faults; to judge others in the areas of their weakness. Rather, the Bible clearly spells out that we must judge ourselves first. However, it teaches that if we see a brother sinning, we are to graciously and sensitively approach that person, "speaking the truth in love" (Eph. 4:15). In fact, our only motive should be love.

The body will build itself up in love when we confess our sins to each other and pray for each other (Jas. 5:16). Some Christians have woefully misconstrued what James means in this passage. They feel they must confess every sin publicly—to the whole body—and with every degree of regularity. This interpretation, of course, leads to unhealthy motives, both for confessing *and* listening! There are some sins that should be confessed only to God,

51

particularly those that do not involve another person. There are other sins that should be confessed only to God and to the person or persons against whom we have sinned. And in some rare instances, there are sins that should be confessed to the whole body because they are sins against the whole body and have hurt the testimony of the whole body.

With these qualifications, we are to confess our sins to one another and pray for one another. It is only as we develop this kind of openness and honesty with other members of the body of Christ that we, as a body, will build outselves up in love!

THE TWENTIETH-CENTURY CHURCH

What happens to a child who is born into this world and is left by himself? I read once of such an event. Cruel parents kept a child isolated for a number of years in a very restricted environment. Lack of proper nourishment, no learning opportunities, and no physical exercise produced an "oversized infant." He lacked proper nourishment and exercise but he still continued to grow physically—though unnaturally; his movements were terribly mechanical and uncoordinated. In fact, he couldn't even walk. But he did not grow mentally, emotionally, nor, of course, spiritually.

Though an unpleasant illustration, it's a graphic picture of some twentieth-century churches. Yes, they grow *physically!* In fact, they get bigger and bigger! But they remain in a state of infancy. Yes, they may be united to the Head, Jesus Christ, with all of the potential for being built up in love. But because of lack of nourishment and exercise they are still in an infant stage. This is a tragedy!

Then too there are some churches that are united to

Jesus Christ through conversion and even have a good diet from the Scriptures. But can you imagine what happens to a child who gorges himself with every degree of regularity, but never gets any exercise?

The picture is clear. To grow properly, a local body of believers must not only have a good diet from the Word of God, but every part of the body must function. And proper body function not only reflects love, it also generates *more love!*

ACTION STEP

What about *your* church? Look over the following biblical directives. Put a (+) by those you sense are priorities in your church. Put a (−) by those you feel are neglected. Put a (0) by those you are not sure about.

1. Each part is doing its work (Eph 4:16). ____
2. Equal concern is expressed for each other ____ (1 Cor. 12:25).
3. We are serving one another in love (Gal. ____ 5:13).
4. We are bearing with each other in love (Eph. ____ 4:2).
5. We are carrying each other's burdens (Gal. ____ 6:2).
6. We are encouraging each other and building ____ each other up (1 Thess. 5:11).
7. We are submitting to one another out of rev- ____ erence for Christ (Eph. 5:21).
8. We are forgiving one another (Eph. 4:32). ____
9. We are being honest with each other (Col. ____ 3:9).
10. We are offering hospitality to one another ____ without grumbling (1 Pet. 4:9).

53

11. We are teaching and counseling one another _____ with all wisdom (Col. 3:16).
12. We are confessing our sins to each other _____ and praying for each other (Jas. 5:16).

Now that you have evaluated your church in the area of body function, evaluate yourself. Read over the list again. What are you doing to contribute even more to the strengths of your church? And what are you doing to help overcome the weaknesses? Circle those you feel you are neglecting, and then write out one thing you can do, beginning today, to help your church grow in love.

Today I will

Note: Most of these directives are not necessarily related to a program of some sort and how you fit into it. Rather, they focus on individual responsibility and spontaneous action within the body of Christ. In other words, you need not wait for someone to ask you to serve in some capacity. You can begin today because Jesus Christ has already asked you to serve His body.

FAMILY OR GROUP PROJECT

Make a continued study of these directives. Share your own evaluations with other members of your family or group. Spend time discussing and praying about how you as a family or group can contribute even more to the functioning body of Christ in your church.

---

[1]The Bible teaches that the elders *are* pastors. And interestingly, nowhere in the New Testament do we have reference to only one elder or one pastor in a local church. The goal for a New Testament church was a plurality of leaders.

chapter 5

LOVE—
THE BRIDGE
TO THE WORLD

"The greatest of these is love!" exclaimed Paul—not only because it builds up the body of Christ, but also because it reaches out to the unsaved. In fact, it's the bridge to the world!

When Jesus charged His disciples to "love one another" (John 13:34), He had in mind the very purpose for which He came to earth. Thus He followed the command to love with a dynamic expectation: "All men will know that you are my disciples if you love one another" (John 13:35).

Jesus Christ came to save a lost world. This He stated very clearly one day to a tax collector named Zacchaeus, "The Son of Man came to seek and to save what was lost" (Luke 19:10). And *love* in His followers was to be the bridge between Christ and the lost.

Love produces unity! This we've already seen from previous chapters. Jesus clarified this truth further in His prayer to the Father shortly before He went to the cross. He prayed earnestly, "May they be brought to complete unity to let the world know that you sent me and have loved them even as you have loved me" (John 17:23).

Dr. Francis Schaeffer calls this truth the "final apologetic," that is, the ultimate and most significant defense for the Christian faith. How can Christians *prove* to the non-Christian world that Jesus Christ is who He claimed to be? To paraphrase what Jesus said, "They'll know we're Christians by our love!" And the unity that love produces is the divine means that God uses to communicate to the world that Jesus Christ was "in the beginning," that He "was with God," that He "was God," and that He "became flesh and lived for a while among us" (John 1:1,2,14).

In some marvelous and mysterious way, every local, loving, functioning and unified body of Christ becomes a powerful witness, demonstrating this truth.

The incarnation surrounds, undergirds, and impregnates the Christian gospel! If Christ were not God, the Christian religion would be, in essence, no different from any other major world religion. All have their leaders, but none have the credentials of Jesus Christ! Because He was *one with God,* He could become the *God-man!* He was *truly* "the Lamb of God, who takes away the sins of the world!" (John 1:29).

GOD'S PLAN IN PERSPECTIVE

When Jesus Christ walked among men He performed many miracles. In Cana, He changed the water into wine. Later, He came back to Cana and healed the nobleman's son while the boy was yet in Capernaum. In Jerusaleum,

He miraculously straightened a man's crooked limbs—a man who had been crippled for thirty-eight years. Across the Sea of Galilee, He fed five thousand men, besides women and children, with five small loaves and two fishes. When he returned to the other side, He walked on the water and calmed the stormy sea. Back in Jerusalem, He made a man see who had been blind from birth. And just a short distance away in the small town of Bethany, He worked one of His greatest miracles—He raised a man from the dead! Lazarus had been in the tomb for four days and yet at the voice of the Son of God, he came forth.

Jesus worked these miracles, and many more, to demonstrate who He was—God come down to live among men. In fact, the apostle John described these very miracles in his gospel so that we might "believe that Jesus is the Christ, the Son of God, and that by believing you [and I] may have life in his name" (John 20:30).

But then Jesus, as a man, left this earth. He went back to heaven. And then for a time, through the power of the Holy Spirit, He gave certain men the same supernatural power. Apostles like Peter, John, and Paul stand out as men who did the same works as Jesus. Many unnamed Christians were also able to work miracles in order to verify the Christian message. Thus the writer of the Hebrew letter said: "This salvation, which was first announced by the Lord, was confirmed to us by those who heard him. God also testified to it by signs, wonders and various miracles, and gifts of the Holy Spirit distributed according to his will" (Heb. 2:3).

But once these signs and gifts had served their purpose—to verify the message of Christ—they subsided. "Where there are prophecies, they will cease," wrote Paul; "Where there are tongues, they will be stilled; where there is knowledge, it will pass away." But, exclaimed Paul, "Love never fails!" And then he culminated this with a profound statement: "And now these three remain: faith, hope and love. But *the greatest of these is love!*" (See 1 Cor. 13:8-13.) Love, in God's divine plan, constitutes the one main thing that will continue to verify the gospel of Christ, even after miracles cease, and until Christ comes again. And this message is what shapes the content of the New Testament letters. This is why there is such a strong emphasis on love and unity throughout all of the epistles written to first-century churches. Love which produces unity is to be the *bridge to the world!* Expressions of love by every member of Christ's body build up the church. This we've clearly demonstrated in the previous chapter. But this love also becomes a *corporate witness* to non-Christians. Equal concern among members of the body, self-sacrificing service to others, bearing with one another and carrying one another's burdens, mutual encouragement, submission, a forgiving spirit, honesty, hospitality, and building up one another through mutual teaching and counseling—all of these expressions of love serve to bear a vigorous and authoritative witness to non-Christians. Inherent in what they see is what their hearts have been longing for ever since they were born. No man can unequivocally deny that there is a yearning to be a part of a community of love.

SOME DIVINE INJUNCTIONS

There are some biblical injunctions given to Christians that bear directly on our witness to the world. And all of these directives relate to the concept of love as it is broadly defined in Scripture. Remember, *Christlikeness* and *love* are synonymous!

• "Make it your ambition to lead a quiet life, to mind

your own business and to work with your own hands, just as we told you, so that your daily life may win the respect of outsiders and so that you will not be dependent on anybody" (1 Thess. 4:11,12).

At first glance, you may have difficulty relating this statement to *love.* But it is really *love in action* in the body, and toward the world.

Evidently, some of the Thessalonian Christians were not demonstrating a loving attitude toward each other. They were creating disturbances, getting into each other's private affairs, and taking advantage of each other materially. This, implied Paul, will *never* "win the respect of outsiders." In other words, non-Christians will reject their life-style. And in rejecting their life-style they will reject their Saviour!

● "All who are under the yoke of slavery should consider their masters worthy of full respect, so that God's name and our teaching may not be slandered" (1 Tim. 6:1).

Most Christians today, particularly in our Western culture, do not face the same problems as those faced by New Testament believers. Here Paul is dealing with the problem of slavery. A number of those who were saved were in bondage to non-Christian masters. In writing to these Christians Paul did not attack slavery *per se.* Rather, he instructed these believers to *respect* their masters and to honor them; to even carry out their tasks with greater diligence and conscientiousness (Eph. 6:5; Col. 3:22; Titus 2:9,10; 1 Pet. 2:18).

Paul also made very clear his reason for advocating this kind of behavior, "that God's name and our teaching may not be slandered." These slaves were to bear a strong witness for Jesus Christ. Their masters were to learn about Christ and see the reality of His presence by seeing it exemplified in the lives of their slaves who had professed Christianity.

There's a great lesson in this injunction for all Christians. We may not be slaves, but many of us are employees! And if we have any witness at all, our employers know we're Christians. And they are watching our lives to see if what we profess makes a difference in our performance! And that difference, the way of love, may be the means whereby they will open their hearts to the message of Jesus Christ and invite Him to be their personal Saviour.

• "So whether you eat or drink or whatever you do, do it all for the glory of God. Do not cause anyone to stumble, whether Jews, Greeks or the church of God—even as I try to please everybody in every way. For I am not seeking my own good but the good of many, so that they may be saved" (1 Cor. 10:31-33).

Everything Christians do is to be done to honor and glorify Jesus Christ. Though it is not always possible to accomplish it, our goal should be to "please everybody in every way." Then Paul spells out why this was his goal—"For I am not seeking my own good but the good of many, *so that they may be saved.*"

Don't misunderstand! Paul is not advocating compromise and inconsistency. He is not suggesting that we tickle people's ears with truth, saying what they want to hear, and doing what they want us to do. Paul never compromised the message of Christ. What he is saying is the same thing he wrote to the Roman Christians: "If it is possible, as far as it depends on you, live at peace with everyone" (Rom. 12:18). In other words, don't say things and do things that would cause others to stumble over the message of Christ and ultimately reject it because of our selfish and self-centered behavior.

• "Live such good lives among the pagans that, though they accuse you of doing wrong, they may see your good deeds and glorify God on the day he visits us" (1 Pet. 2:12).

This is a forceful injunction. Many of the New Testament Christians were being falsely accused of immorality and other sins. Peter, in identifying with their plight, exhorted them to defend their life-style by continuing to live consistently for Jesus Christ. Someday, he implied, your accusers may acknowledge the truth. For if they are honest at all, they cannot continue to malign the Christian when they see that he can handle even false accusations with Christian poise and non-defensiveness.

Sometimes non-Christians purposely put Christians to the test to see if we are real. And they know that false accusations, though a very low blow to any person, will soon prove how strong we really are in our commitment to live like Christ, the One who, "when they hurled their insults at him, he did not retaliate; when he suffered, he made no threats. Instead, he entrusted himself to who judges justly" (1 Pet. 2:23).

Peter's primary concern was for the "pagan's" salvation. Thus, he says, this kind of life-style may eventually bring people to Jesus Christ. "They may see your good deeds and glorify God on the day he visits us." They may respond to the gospel when the Holy Spirit is working in their hearts.

It was Jesus who instituted this concept for winning people to Himself when He said, "Let your light shine before men, that they may see your good deeds and praise your Father in heaven" (Matt. 5:16).

• "Wives, in the same way be submissive to your husbands so that, if any of them do not believe the word, they may be won over without talk by the behavior of their wives, when they see the purity and reverence of your lives" (1 Pet. 3:1,2).

Here Peter was speaking to women whose husbands had not yet professed faith in Jesus Christ. How might they win their husbands to Jesus Christ? Certainly not by verbal bombardments! Rather, they were to be submissive, that is, unselfish in their behavior. They were to demonstrate "purity" and "reverence." Their life-style was to reflect a "gentle and quiet spirit" (1 Pet. 3:4). Peter is saying that there is dynamic power in Christlike behavior, in true biblical love. It is the bridge to the world—in this case to the unsaved husbands.

Many twentieth-century Christian wives, who are married to non-Christians, can learn a very significant lesson from Peter's instructions. It is a mistake to actively preach *at* your husband, to persistently tell him he's lost and needs to repent.

And what makes it doubly devastating is when you let him know that you learned all this from a sensitive, understanding, wonderful pastor at the new church you've been attending.

What will affect him and soften his heart toward the gospel? It's seeing a changed life, as though he were living with a different person, experiencing a submissive spirit—all of which reflect true biblical love.

• "I urge, then, first of all, that requests, prayers, intercessions and thanksgiving be made for everyone—for kings and all those in authority, that we may live peaceful and quiet lives in all godliness and holiness. This is good, and pleases God our Savior, who wants all men to be saved and come to a knowledge of the truth" (1 Tim. 2:1-4).

In this passage we often neglect to focus on why Paul was concerned about praying for everyone, particularly for government officials. And why he desired a peaceful environment in which to live for Christ! "This is good," he said, because God "wants all men to be saved."

Two things stand out boldly in this injunction. First, non-Christians, especially people who are responsible for civic affairs, are affected by people who pray for them. This is true, not only from a divine perspective, but also from a human perspective. As human beings, they cannot help but be impressed with this act of love.

Second, their decisions regarding government laws and policies may be affected positively, that is, they may make decisions favoring Christians rather than making decisions that bring persecution. An environment reflecting persecution often destroys the freedom to share Christ with others.

How much do we pray for our government officials? And how many of them *know* that we are praying for them? How about sitting down today and writing a letter to your mayor, your governor, your congressman, and even to the President of the United States, telling them that we are asking God to give them unusual wisdom to be able to make correct decisions in these difficult days.

• "Be wise in the way you act toward outsiders; make the most of every opportunity. Let your conversation be always full of grace, seasoned with salt, so that you may know how to answer everyone" (Col. 4:5,6).

A life-style demonstrating Christ's love opens up many doors for casual conversation. No one can be saved by simply *seeing* Christians love each other! They must know *why* Christians act that way.

The answer, of course, is Jesus Christ and what He has done for mankind. By believing in Him, by receiving Him as a personal Saviour, by inviting Him into our lives, we are changed and enabled to "love out" His love. This is the message of the gospel.

Paul was concerned that the Colossian Christians make the most of every opportunity to share a verbal witness for Christ. And he was also concerned that they share Christ appropriately. As they spoke they were to reflect the grace of God. Their words were to be "seasoned with salt," that is, palatable to the hearers. They were to develop the ability to answer *everyone* with a sweet spirit, reflecting the love of Jesus Christ.

• "But in your hearts acknowledge Christ as the holy Lord. Always be prepared to give an answer to everyone who asks you to give the reason for the hope that you have. But do this with gentleness and respect, keeping a clear conscience, so that those who speak maliciously against your good behavior in Christ may be ashamed of their slander" (1 Pet. 3:15,16).

Peter's concern was the same as Paul's. Christians are to always be ready to share Christ, especially when others ask why we are so confident and sure of our salvation.

Not all, of course, will respond to the explanation or to the invitation to receive Christ. But as we share we should never give people a reason to attack our attitude or the spirit in which we have communicated. Like Paul, Peter warned that we must share with "gentleness and respect." Furthermore, whether or not we feel free—have a "clear conscience"—to share Christ with those who know us, is a good test of how successfully we are living Christ's life before them. If we're ashamed to share Christ, perhaps our life-style has violated His.

THE TWENTIETH-CENTURY CHURCH

The study of evangelism and how it happened in first-century churches reveals some very helpful principles that will guide us in reaching twentieth-century people for Christ.

First, evangelism must begin in our own communities.

New Testament Christians began in Jerusalem, then moved out to Judea, Samaria, and the uttermost part of the earth. And as churches were established in various communities, Christians were instructed to live like Jesus Christ in every human relationship so as to be able to share the gospel of Christ forcefully.

Frequently, local churches neglect their own communities. A virile foreign missions program becomes a substitute for local outreach. Missionary budgets replace on-the-spot evangelistic activity. Overseas missionaries, supported by the church, become a substitute for engaging in local evangelism.

This ought not to be! There is no excuse for a local church neglecting its own "Jerusalem." The field is the world, of course, but the world begins in our own backyard, or across the street. This was the story of New Testament believers.

Don't misunderstand! I'm not talking exclusively about the community around the "church building." That's part of it! But the most significant community is the one in which you live as an individual or as a family. Every home, particularly, should reflect the church in miniature by reaching out in love and concern for those around you.

Second, corporate or "body" evangelism is foundational to effective personal evangelism. In the New Testament, the functioning and loving body of Christ set the stage for individual witness. Personal evangelism happens naturally when it develops out of a context of love and unity in a body of believers. Personal witness takes on unusual significance against the backdrop of mature

Christians who are making an impact in their communities because of their integrity, their unselfish behavior, their orderly conduct, their wisdom, their diligence, their humility and yet their forthright testimony for Jesus Christ.

Third, simply loving each other as Christians and loving non-Christians is not enough! We must also explain the gospel of Christ sensitively but clearly. Many Christians feel our responsibility stops when we have developed a visual Christian life-style. But the gospel can only be understood when it is verbalized. Love is only the bridge! Love and unity prepare the way. They are the means to our end, that of sharing the message of Christ in a clear and understandable way.

Here again is the genius of Scripture! If the Bible had given absolute methods for sharing Christ, the Holy Spirit would have "locked us in" to the first-century culture. We need to develop our own methods, based on New Testament principles, to enable us to share Christ with the twentieth-century person. Christians are to be "prepared to give an answer to everyone," not only in the first century, but also in the twentieth.

Thus God gives us injunctions to live for Christ and to share Christ. And He desires that we develop a methodology that will work at any given moment in history and in any given situation and culture.

ACTION STEP

There is no one way to share Christ verbally. But there are various methods that have been recently developed to help us. No doubt one of the most widely used methods is that developed by Campus Crusade for Christ—the *Four Spiritual Laws* booklet. Another one is *How to Have a Happy and Meaningful Life* by Dallas Theological

Seminary. There is also the "Navigator" approach or the "Kennedy" approach or the "New Life Technique." Others could be named.

The important thing is that we have a method at our disposal, a simple and gracious way to share Christ, and then be available for God to use us. It is also important that we recognize that these are only tools, twentieth-century methods designed to reach twentieth-century people. Consequently, we must be prepared to adapt these methods or to even change these methods if they do not work in certain situations. But the primary objective must always be in view—to share Christ clearly, effectively, and above all, in love!

GROUP OR FAMILY PROJECT

As a family, plan to attend a special seminar to learn how to share Christ effectively. For example, the Campus Crusade Lay Institute for Evangelism is an excellent opportunity for the whole family. You may wish to write to Campus Crusade for Christ, Arrowhead Springs, San Bernardino, California, 92404, and ask them when a lay institute will be conducted in your area.

chapter 6

HOPE—
HOW IT CAN
BE RECOGNIZED

We're living in a world of uncertainty! Everywhere prophets of doom are crying out their foreboding messages. Some warn of an impending worldwide economic crisis. Others are desperately concerned about the prospect of an eventual depletion of our natural resources leading to a worldwide famine and starvation. Still others believe that pollution will eventually emerge as the destroyer. Some are writing and speaking even more dramatically about earthquakes that will slide whole cities into the sea, or a nuclear holocaust that will destroy millions of lives and send the world back to the Dark Ages.

Though most of these voices crying in the wilderness vary in their particular predictions, they are all, including non-Christians, correct in one respect. Ultimate destruction and world disaster is coming! Exactly when, we do not know. But it is coming! How related it will be to what is now happening is an uncertainty. Many believe that the present world crises are building towards a great culmination—the second coming of Jesus Christ to bring judgment on unbelieving mankind.

Regardless of what happens or when, Christians should not be fearful of God's final judgment. We are not like those who are "without hope and without God in the world" (Eph. 2:12). True, Paul has told us that "destruction will come on them [non-Christians] suddenly, as labor pains on a pregnant woman, and they will not escape" (1 Thess. 5:3). But he also hurried to inform the Thessalonian Christians that this day would not surprise them. "For," said Paul, "God did not appoint us to suffer wrath but to receive salvation through our Lord Jesus Christ" (1 Thess. 5:9).

But hope for the Christian is not only related to ultimate deliverance from God's wrath, it also involves God's strength and help in the midst of present problems. Paul referred to this hope when he was in a Roman prison. Uncertain about his future, he wrote to the Philippians with great confidence—"I eagerly expect and hope that I will in no way be ashamed, but will have sufficient courage so that now as always Christ will be exalted in my body, whether by life or by death" (Phil. 1:20).

A mature body of Christians reflects this hope. They know with certainty that they will be sustained in the trials of daily living and that they will someday be saved and delivered from this world. And they rejoice in that hope!

When Paul measured the maturity level of a local church he looked first of all for love. As we've seen, love stands out as the greatest mark of maturity. Love reflects Christ's life. It causes the body to function and to build itself up. And when it is present it becomes a dynamic bridge to the world—a means to open hearts and lives to the gospel.

But hope is also important in measuring the maturity level of a church. As we've seen in chapter one, Paul spoke of it often when writing to the New Testament churches. When he was pleased with their progress in this area, he thanked God for the hope that was evident in their midst (Col. 1:4,5; 1 Thess. 1:2,3).

Like love, hope is also visible! When it is there, it is obvious to both Christians and non-Christians. "Always be prepared," wrote Peter, "to give an answer to everyone who asks you to give the reason for the hope that you have" (1 Pet. 3:15). It is clear, of course, that the reason people ask about hope is that they recognize it, they see it, they are impressed by it! It does not take a person without hope long to recognize people with hope.

How then can Christian hope be specifically recognized? How is it reflected by a mature body of believers?

HOPE REFLECTS FAITH IN A FUTURE RESURRECTION

Christian hope and the concept of a future resurrection from the dead are synonymous. Without this doctrine there can be no real Christian point of view. To claim to be a Christian and at the same time deny a literal resurrection is contradictory.

The concept of hope first appears in the New Testament in the book of Acts. Significantly, the word is used by the apostle Peter in his first sermon on the day of Pentecost to describe Christ's attitude about His own death. Speaking to those who had crucified the Lord, he quoted from one of David's messianic psalms: "Therefore my heart is glad and my tongue rejoices; my body also will live in hope, because you will not abandon me to the grave, nor will you let your Holy One undergo decay" (Acts 2:26,27).

As you trace the doctrine of the resurrection in the Bible, it becomes very clear that *because Christ lives, we too shall live*. It is because of His resurrection that we too claim the promise that someday we shall also be raised. Paul made this very clear in his first letter to the Corinthians. Listen to his logic: "For if the dead are not raised, then Christ has not been raised either. And if Christ has not been raised, your faith is futile; you are still in your sins. Then those also who have fallen asleep in Christ are lost. If only for this life we have hope in Christ, we are to be pitied more than all men. But Christ has indeed been raised from the dead, the first-fruits of those who have fallen asleep" (1 Cor. 15:16-20).

Following are some additional Scriptures that make specific reference to *hope* in relationship to the resurrection.

Paul Before the Sanhedrin

"Then Paul, knowing that some of them were Sadducees and the others Pharisees, called out in the Sanhedrin, 'My brothers, I am a Pharisee, the son of a Pharisee. I stand on trial because of my *hope* in the resurrection of the dead' " (Acts 23:6).

Paul Before Felix

"I have the same *hope* in God as these men, that there will be a resurrection of both the righteous and the wicked" (Acts 24:15).

Paul Before Agrippa

"And now it is because of my *hope* in what God has

promised our fathers that I am on trial today. This is the promise our twelve tribes are *hoping* to see fulfilled as they earnestly serve God day and night. Your Majesty, it is because of this *hope* that the Jews are accusing me. Why should any of you consider it incredible that God raises the dead?" (Acts 26:6-8).

Paul's Letter to the Romans

"But we ourselves, who have the firstfruits of the Spirit, groan inwardly as we wait eagerly for our adoption as sons, the redemption of our bodies. For in this hope we were saved" (Rom. 8:23,24).

Paul's Letter to the Thessalonians

"Brothers, we do not want you to be ignorant about those who sleep, or to grieve like the rest of men, who have no *hope.* We believe that Jesus died and rose again and so we believe that God will bring with Jesus those who sleep in him" (1 Thess. 4:13,14).

Peter's Letter to Various Churches

"Praise be to the God and Father of our Lord Jesus Christ! In his great mercy he has given us new birth into a living hope through the resurrection of Jesus Christ from the dead, and into an inheritance that can never perish, spoil or fade—kept in heaven for you" (1 Pet. 1:3,4).

HOPE REFLECTS AN ASSURANCE OF ETERNAL SALVATION

To be sure, faith in a future resurrection and assurance of eternal salvation are inseparable concepts. But the person uninitiated in the finer parts of Christian theology may ask, "Resurrected for what?" The answer, of course, is that we will be resurrected to enter a new life with a new body—one that defies space and time limitations. Eternal life, of course, begins the moment a person truly puts his faith in Jesus Christ (John 3:36). And if we die before Christ comes, "to be away from the body" is to be "at home with the Lord" (2 Cor. 5:8). But eternal life in a "new body" begins the moment Christ comes, both for those who are yet alive and for those who have died. (See 1 Cor. 15:50-54; 1 Thess. 4:13-18.) And, said Paul, "We will be with the Lord forever" (1 Thess. 4:17).

Mature Christians have this hope and demonstrate an assurance that they will never die. Physically, yes! But spiritually, no! Though death may knock at their door, it is only a stepping stone to a new life that will never end. Thus a funeral for a Christian, though sad from a human perspective, can be a joyful occasion. The one who has died has entered an eternal existence that is free from pain, sorrow, and all of the other vicissitudes of this life.

The following Scriptures express this hope in various ways:

The Hope of Glory

"Therefore, since we have been justified through faith, we have peace with God through our Lord Jesus Christ, through whom we have gained access by faith into this grace in which we now stand. And we rejoice in the *hope of the glory of God*" (Rom. 5:1,2).

"To them God has chosen to make known among the Gentiles the glorious riches of this mystery, which is Christ in you, *the hope of glory*" (Col. 1:27).

"He called you to this through our gospel, that you might share in the glory of our Lord Jesus Christ. . . . May our Lord Jesus Christ himself and God our Father, who loved us and by his grace gave us eternal encouragement and *good hope,* encourage and strengthen you in every good deed and word" (2 Thess. 2:14,16,17).

The Hope of Salvation

"But you, brothers, are not in darkness so that this day should surprise you like a thief. You are all sons of the light and sons of the day. We do not belong to the night or to the darkness. . . . But since we belong to the day, let us be self-controlled, putting on faith and love as a breastplate, and the *hope of salvation* as a helmet" (1 Thess. 5:4,5,8).

The Hope of Eternal Life

"But when the kindness and love of God our Savior appeared, he saved us, not because of righteous things we had done, but because of his mercy. He saved us through the washing of rebirth and renewal by the Holy Spirit, whom he poured out on us generously through Jesus Christ our Savior, so that, having been justified by his grace, we might become heirs having the *hope of eternal life*" (Titus 3:4-7).

A Living Hope

"Praise be to the God and Father of our Lord Jesus Christ! In his great mercy he has given us new birth into a *living hope* through the resurrection of Jesus Christ from the dead, and into an inheritance that can never perish, spoil or fade—kept in heaven for you." (1 Pet. 1:3,4).

HOPE PRODUCES GODLY LIVING IN VIEW OF CHRIST'S SECOND COMING

Two men of God in the first century were greatly

concerned about this concept. John, often called the apostle of love, clearly stressed holiness of life in light of the return of Christ. Listen to his argument: "Dear friends, now we are children of God," that is, we have eternal life right now! He continued, "And what we will be has not yet been made known. But we *know* that when he appears, we shall be like him, for we shall see him as he is." And then the apostle concludes his argument with this measure of concern—"Everyone who has *this hope* in him [the hope of being like Christ] purifies himself, just as he is pure" (1 John 3:2,3).

Paul, in his letter to Titus, dealt with the same issue. He also pleaded for Godly and righteous living "while we wait for the *blessed hope*—the glorious appearing of our great God and Savior, Jesus Christ." And why this emphasis on holiness? Because Jesus Christ "gave himself for us to redeem us from all wickedness and to purify for himself a people that are his very own, eager to do what is good" (Titus 2:11-14).

A body of believers, then, which has *hope* and lives in the light of that *hope* will reflect the life of Jesus Christ. And since Christlikeness is the essence of love, we see again that *hope produces love.* This is one reason why Paul says love is the greatest! Where true love is, there is also hope! In fact, hope is foundational to love. You cannot have one without the other!

WHERE THERE IS HOPE
THERE IS DOCTRINAL STABILITY

The Thessalonian Church

When Paul wrote his first letter to the church at Thessalonica he thanked God for their "endurance inspired by *hope* in our Lord Jesus Christ" (1 Thess. 1:3). These

Christians faced severe suffering because of their faith in Christ. But in spite of the persecution they "welcomed the message" of salvation. In fact, Paul commended them for being a "model to all the believers in Macedonia and Achaia" (1 Thess. 1:6,7).

Here was a New Testament church that demonstrated endurance and steadfastness because of their view of the future, because of their *hope!* In fact, Paul wrote that because of their hope people everywhere were talking about how these pagan people had "turned to God from idols to serve the living and true God, and to wait for his Son from heaven" (1 Thess. 1:9).

The Roman Church

Interestingly, Paul reversed the process when he wrote to the believers in Rome. In this case, he told them that hope would be developed because of suffering. Having written about hope that accompanies salvation (Rom. 5:1,2), he then went on to say, "Not only so, but we also rejoice in our sufferings, because we know that suffering produces perseverance; perseverance, character; and character, *hope*" (Rom. 5:3,4). In other words, salvation or hope produces endurance. But suffering and trials will also develop that hope.

The Hebrew Christians

The writer of the Hebrew epistle was also concerned about the relationship between stability and hope. Thus he wrote: "We have this *hope* as an anchor for the soul, firm and secure" (Heb. 6:19). God does not intend for His children to be "tossed back and forth by the waves, and blown here and there by every wind of teaching and by the cunning and craftiness of men in their deceitful scheming" (Eph. 4:14). That is why the author of the

76

Hebrews wrote: "Let us hold unswervingly to the *hope* we profess" (Heb. 10:23). And that is why Paul wrote to Timothy—"Command those who are rich in this present world not . . . to put their *hope* in wealth, which is so uncertain, but to put their *hope* in God" (1 Tim. 6:17).

HOPE REFLECTS JOY

Joy is perhaps one of the most visible evidences of hope in a mature body of Christians. Hope produces joy!

This was one of Paul's great concerns for the Roman Christians. They were not enjoying their salvation as they should. And Paul admonished them to do so!

Earlier in the epistle he wrote, "We *rejoice* in the hope of the glory of God" (Rom. 5:2). Later he said, "Be *joyful* in hope" (Rom. 12:12). And finally, he concluded his epistle with a prayer: "May the God of hope fill you with great *joy* and peace as you trust in him, so that you may overflow with hope by the power of the Holy Spirit" (Rom. 15:13).

New Testament Christians who really understood their position in Christ showed it. They rejoiced—even in the midst of trials and tribulations. They understood that these difficulties and stressful experiences would produce even more maturity in their lives. Thus James wrote: "Consider it pure *joy,* my brothers, whenever you face trials of many kinds, because you know that the testing of your faith develops perseverance. Perseverance must finish its work so that you may be mature and complete, not lacking anything" (Jas. 1:2-4).

HOPE REFLECTS BOLDNESS
IN APPROACHING GOD

In Old Testament days, any man approaching God

had to do so very cautiously. God is a holy God and because of His holiness, men could not approach Him directly. Consequently, a system of ritual, sacrifice, and mediators was instituted to enable Israel to approach God and to enjoy His presence. Only the high priest could enter the holy of holies in the Tabernacle in order to approach God directly. In fact, some who violated these laws were struck dead!

But Jesus Christ has changed all that! He became our perfect sacrifice and opened a new way to God. Consequently, we have "confidence to enter the Most Holy Place by the blood of Jesus." We now have "a new and living way opened for us." And "since we have a great priest over the house of God" we can "draw near to God with a sincere heart in full assurance of faith" (Heb. 10:19-22). Paul wrote to the Corinthians, "Since we have such a *hope,* we are very bold" (2 Cor. 3:12).

One of the most significant evidences of hope is when Christians approach God—reverently, yes, but without fear. How tremendous to be able to call Him Father! How wonderful to be able to open our hearts before Him! How exciting to be able to pray to Him directly! We need no human mediator. We need no earthly priest to go before us. We can boldly enter His presence ourselves. Why? Because now "there is one God and one mediator between God and men, the man Christ Jesus" (1 Tim. 2:5).

THE TWENTIETH-CENTURY CHURCH

I grew up in a church that probably illustrates the absence of hope about as well as the Corinthian church illustrates the absence of love. Though we all believed in a coming resurrection and a second coming of Christ, we were not taught that we could look forward to these events with joy. Why? Because we didn't believe we could be sure that we would inherit eternal life until we were measured by our works at the judgment seat of God.

I remember—*how* I remember—struggling with the assurance of my salvation. I thought I was saved one day and lost the next. My joy was dependent on my feelings, which were mostly negative. In those days my life could be generaly chracterized by the word "instability." And what was even more tragic, the whole church reflected the same attitude and behavior, and still does.

I remember, too, how fearful I was to approach God. Somehow I always felt that people who did the most "good works" were the ones God accepted. Consequently, I found myself trying to pay for my own sins—even after I became a Christian.

How unfortunate! Yes! But how wonderful to know the truth and to be able to speak "the truth in love" (Eph. 4:15). How gratifying to be able to help other Christians in the twentieth century to *know* that they have eternal life! How exciting to be a part of a body of Christians that is growing—not only in *love,* but *hope!*

ACTION STEP

Use the following five-point scale to measure your own church in the light of the biblical criteria for hope. Circle the number that best represents your point of view.

1. Our church demonstrates faith in a future resurrection.

Weak   1   2   3   4   5   Strong

2. Our church demonstrates an assurance of eternal salvation.

Weak   1   2   3   4   5   Strong

3. Our church demonstrates that we are living holy lives in the light of Christ's second coming.

Weak   1   2   3   4   5   Strong

4. Our church demonstrates doctrinal stability.

Weak   1   2   3   4   5   Strong

5. Our church demonstrates joy.

Weak   1   2   3   4   5   Strong

6. Our church demonstrates boldness in approaching God.

Weak   1   2   3   4   5   Strong

A local church, of course, is made up of individual Christians. How, then do you personally measure up to this biblical criteria that reflect hope? Measure yourself in the light of what you observe generally in the body at large. Underscore the number that best represents your personal maturity in these six areas.

Now that you have isolated your areas of strength and weaknesses, what are you going to do about it? (Clue: Generally, the answer is a better understanding of Scripture.) What goal can you set up for yourself that will help you learn more about the Word of God?

FAMILY OR GROUP PROJECT

Use the five-point scale to measure the maturity level of your own family. Review each concept related to hope and then have each family member evaluate the family as a whole. Then have each family member evaluate his or her own life personally. Spend time in discussion and prayer regarding future family goals that will help all of you grow spiritually in the area of hope.

NOTE: If you're single, think in terms of a small group of Christians with whom you have close fellowship and work through the same process.

chapter 7

HOPE—
AND THE CHURCH
AT EPHESUS

Hope is a mark of Christian maturity in a body of Christians. Though it has various facets and can be recognized in various ways, it can be succinctly summarized as doctrinal insight and stability, particularly in respect to our present and future relationship with God through Jesus Christ. Paul's letter to the Ephesians and particularly his prayer for them point to a body of believers who had yet to mature in this area of their Christian lives.

As noted previously, Paul looked for *faith, hope,* and *love* when measuring the maturity level of a church. The Colossians illustrate a church that had matured significantly in all three of these areas (Col. 1:3,4) When Paul wrote to the Thessalonians in his first letter he also thanked God for their maturity in these three areas; their "work produced by faith," their "labor prompted by love," and their "endurance inspired by hope" (1 Thess. 1:3).

But when he wrote to the Ephesians he thanked God for their *faith* and *love*, but prayed that the eyes of their hearts might be enlightened so that they might "know the *hope*" to which God had called them (Eph. 1:18).

The words "hope" or "calling" summarize succinctly Paul's thrust and concern in the first three chapters of this letter. Thus we often refer to these chapters as the "doctrinal section" of the Ephesian letter.

The focus of Paul's concern shapes his prayer for these Christians. This prayer appears in two sections of the letter. Although separated by a number of verses these sections represent one prayer.

"For this reason, I, since I heard about your faith in the Lord Jesus and your love for all the saints, have never stopped giving thanks for you, remembering you in my prayers. I keep asking that the God of our Lord Jesus Christ, the glorious Father, may give you the Spirit of wisdom and revelation, so that you may know him better. I pray also that the eyes of your heart may be enlightened in order that you may know the hope to which he has called you, the riches of his glorious inheritance in the saints, and his incomparably great power for us who believe" (Eph. 1:15-19, *NIV*).

"I pray that out of his glorious riches he may strengthen you with power through his Spirit in your inner being, so that Christ may dwell in your hearts through faith. And I pray that you, being rooted and established in love, may have power, together with all the saints, to grasp how wide and long and high and deep is the love of Christ, and to know this love that surpasses knowledge—that you may be filled to the measure of all the fullness of God" (Eph. 3:16-19, *NIV*).

EPHESIANS

1:15 For this reason, I,

since I heard about
- your faith in the Lord Jesus
  and
- your love for all the saints,

16 have never stopped
- giving thanks for you,
- remembering you in my prayers.

17 I keep asking that

the God of our Lord Jesus Christ,
the glorious Father

may give you the

Spirit of wisdom and revelation,
so that you may know him better.

18 I pray also
that the eyes of your heart may be enlightened
in order that you may know

the hope to which he has called you

the riches of his glorious inheritance with the saints,
and
his incomparably great power for us who believe . . .

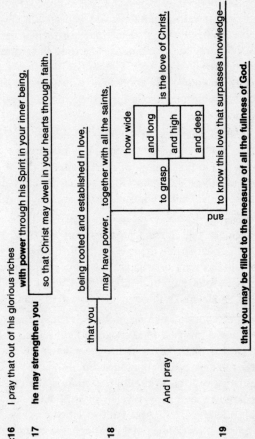

3:16 I pray that out of his glorious riches

with power through his Spirit in your inner being,

17 **he may strengthen you**

so that Christ may dwell in your hearts through faith.

being rooted and established in love,

may have power, together with all the saints,

that you

how wide
and long
and high
and deep

is the love of Christ,

to grasp

18

And I pray

and

to know this love that surpasses knowledge—

19 **that you may be filled to the measure of all the fullness of God.**

KNOW GOD BETTER

Paul prayed that these believers might know God better (1:17).

Paul was concerned that these Christians might mature in hope. And he knew that the way for them to grow in doctrinal insight and stability regarding their present and future relationship with God was to learn *to know God better,* to know more about Him. Consequently, Paul prayed that God might give them the "Spirit of wisdom and revelation."

What Paul meant by the "Spirit of wisdom and revelation" is a matter of opinion. Personally, I believe he was referring to the functioning of special gifts of the Spirit, particularly those gifts that God gave in the early days of the church to enable Christians to know the very mind and thoughts of God.

Remember that these Christians had no New Testament. This letter may have been the first piece of New Testament literature they had ever seen or heard or read. Their only source of truth about God was from God Himself as He spoke through various gifted men.

Paul, of course, was one of those men. He was an apostle and a prophet. God spoke to Paul revealing His great eternal plan. Later in this very letter he wrote: "Surely you have heard about the administration of God's grace that was given to me for you, that is, the mystery made known to me by revelation, as I have already written briefly" (3:2,3). And Paul specified God's intent in giving this revelation, that "through the church, the manifold wisdom of God should be made known . . ." (3:10).

Paul was praying, then, that these Christians might come to know the "glorious Father" better by being exposed to those who were gifted by the Holy Spirit to reveal His eternal plan. And what was that plan? Paul explained it in the next part of his prayer.

BE ENLIGHTENED

Paul prayed that the eyes of their heart might be enlightened (that is, that they might come to know God better)—and for three reasons:

First, that they might know the *hope* to which God had called them (1:18). Chapter two of Ephesians delineates and contrasts two kinds of people, those *without hope* and those *with hope*. Note the following:

THOSE WITHOUT HOPE ARE:	THOSE WITH HOPE ARE:
1. Dead in transgressions and sins (2:1)	1. Made alive with Christ (2:5)
2. Gratifying the cravings of the sinful nature and following its desires and thoughts (2:3)	2. Raised up with Christ and seated with him in the heavenly realms (2:6)
3. By nature—objects of wrath (2:3)	3. By calling—objects of his grace (2:7)
4. Separate from Christ (2:12)	4. Made one with Christ (2:14)
5. Excluded from citizenship in Israel and foreigners to the covenants of the promise (2:12)	5. No longer foreigners and aliens, but fellow citizens with God's people and members of God's household (2:19)
6. Without hope and without God in the world (2:12)	6. A dwelling in which God lives by his spirit (2:22)

What a contrast! Evidently, these New Testament Christians had a strong *faith* in Jesus Christ. And without doubt, they were expressing Christ's *love* toward each other. Otherwise, Paul would not have commended them in these areas. But for some reason, they were not too sure of their present and future position in Christ. Since most of them had been Gentiles converted out of a pagan culture, perhaps there were some pious Christian Jews in the church who were upsetting them, telling them they were still on the "outside looking in." Or perhaps they had been told that they were saved but would always have to occupy a lower place in God's eternal kingdom. After all, the Gentiles were not God's *chosen* people!

But Paul was intent on telling them that he was one Christian Jew who knew the correct story! "I, Paul," he exclaimed, am a "prisoner of Christ Jesus for the sake of you Gentiles" (3:1). Paul had "insight into the mystery of Christ, which was not made known to men in other generations" as it now had been "revealed by the Spirit to God's holy apostles and prophets" (3:4,5).

And what was that mystery? Paul could not have been clearer. "This mystery is that through the gospel the Gentiles are heirs together with Israel, members together of one body, and sharers together in the promise in Christ Jesus" (3:6).

This is no doubt why Paul, in Ephesians 4, was emphatic about the fact that there is only "one body and one Spirit." There is only "one hope"—not one for the Jews and one for the Gentiles. There is only "one Lord, one faith, one baptism; one God and Father of all, who is over all and through all and in all" (4:6).

Second, that they might know the riches of God's glorious inheritance in the saints (1:18).

Christians have an inheritance that surpasses anything

this world could ever imagine or dream of. And unlike any earthly inheritance, ours will "never perish, spoil or fade" (1 Pet. 1:4). It is eternal! And though this message is for both Jew and Gentile, Paul was especially called to "preach to the Gentiles the unsearchable riches of Christ" (Eph. 3:8).

This inheritance—these riches—are spelled out clearly in the introduction of Paul's letter to the Ephesians. Yet they are profound and mind-bending concepts which we will never understand on this side of heaven. God's eternal grace and mercy have been lavished on both Jews and Gentiles. True, Israel represents God's chosen people on earth, but God also has a chosen people from all nations of the earth—the chosen people who will spend eternity with Him. By revelation Paul was given the insight that God "chose us in him [Christ] before the creation of the world" (1:4). Also, God "predestined us to be adopted as sons through Jesus Christ" (1:5), and "in him [Christ] we have redemption through his blood, the forgiveness of sins" (1:7). And when we believed, we were "marked with a seal, the promised Holy Spirit" (1:13).

These are truths that boggle a man's mind. But they are true nevertheless! And when understood correctly they give a Christian fantastic hope. Otherwise, God would not have revealed these truths to us. He did not tell us these things to confuse us, but to strengthen us.

Only immature Christians become confused and frustrated about the sovereignty of God and the free will of man. Either they become "super-sovereigntists," neglecting human responsibility, or they put a "super-emphasis" on man's free will and they neglect God's perspective.

You see, both are true, but you'll never be able to reconcile the two. In fact, we may spend all eternity just coming to understand this one concept. God *is* in control of the universe. His plan *is* on schedule. But man is still responsible for his actions! And every person in the world is a candidate for heaven. God does not want "anyone to perish, but everyone to come to repentance" (2 Pet. 3:9).

When accepted by faith, these concepts give a body of believers both a divine and human perspective on God's plan for their life—a perspective that leads to a strong hope that is manifested by doctrinal insight and stability. "Then," wrote Paul later in his letter, "we will no longer be infants, tossed back and forth by the waves, and blown here and there by every wind of teaching and by the cunning and craftiness of men in their deceitful scheming. Instead, speaking the truth in love, we will in all things grow up into him who is the Head, that is, Christ" (Eph. 4:14,15).

Third, that they might know God's incomparably great power for us who believe (1:19).

What is this power? It is like the working of His mighty strength which he "exerted in Christ when he raised him from the dead and seated him at his right hand in the heavenly realms, far above all rule and authority, power and dominion, and every title that can be given, not only in the present age but also in the one to come" (1:20,21).

And it is this same power that "made us alive with Christ" and "raised us up with Christ and seated us with him in the heavenly realms in Christ Jesus" (2:5,6).

Hope is based on knowledge—knowledge of what Christ has done for us, not only now, but eternally. If God raised Christ from the dead, He can raise us from the dead! And He will. He is the omnipotent God! Do you know that? More specifically, do you believe it? If you do, to the degree you understand and believe, you are coming to know the *hope* to which God has called you!

BE STRENGTHENED

Paul prayed that these Christians might be strengthened right now—in the present (3:16,17).

It is in truly *knowing* our position in Christ and in truly *believing* that we belong to Christ that we tap the power of God for daily Christian living. To know the truth is to be set free (John 8:32)—that is, if we act on that truth! Thus Christ dwells in our hearts through faith. We received Him by faith and we must walk by faith (Col. 2:6). And as we walk day by day in the light of our glorious hope, He will strengthen us with power through His Spirit in our inner being.

BE FILLED WITH GOD

And finally, Paul prayed that these Christians might be filled to the measure of all the fullness of God (3:18,19).

This is the grand culmination of Paul's prayer. He knew they were already walking by *faith.* And he knew they were rooted and established in *love.* This is why in the early part of his letter he commended them for this manifestation of Christian maturity (1:15).

But Paul's great concern for the Ephesians was that they might know the hope to which God had called them. And as we've seen, this could only be developed through understanding the love of God that saved us by His grace, regardless of background or racial heritage. This love, wrote Paul, is beyond human measurement and beyond human knowledge. It involves knowledge that is supernatural and eternal. And that, my friend, is what the Bible is all about!

91

THE TWENTIETH-CENTURY CHURCH

How can Paul's prayer be answered today? In many respects, those of us living in the twentieth century have a much greater advantage than those living in the early days of the church. True, we cannot actually sit at the feet of Paul and listen to him expound the revelation and wisdom of God. But we have an even greater privilege—we can "sit at the feet" of not only Paul and read what he wrote to *many* churches, but we can listen to the great apostle Peter. We can listen to John, who probably knew Jesus Christ more intimately than any other apostle. We can listen to Matthew and Mark and Luke as they unfold their story of the life of Jesus Christ. We can read the letter that James wrote to clarify the relationship between faith and works.

In other words, twentieth-century Christians can know God better than many New Testament Christians. Why? Because we have the completed revelation of God. Here it is, laid out before us, compiled in one book, expressed in dozens of translations, and published in a multitude of languages. Today we have scholars by the thousands who can translate the Scriptures from the original languages. We have presses that can print Bibles by the millions. And we have distribution channels that are helping us to circulate the Scriptures all over the world. In many tribes, the first book that these people ever read is the Bible—thanks to thousands of Christian linguists who are giving their lives to learning a foreign language, teaching the people to read, and then translating the Bible into their own language so they can read it, too.

Is there any excuse for twentieth-century Christians who live in twentieth-century America for not *knowing the hope* to which God has called us? For not knowing how *rich* we really are? For not knowing how great *God's power* really is? For not knowing more and more about *God's marvelous love?* Putting it more directly and succinctly, is there any reason—any excuse—for not being "filled to the measure of all the fullness of God"?

If you're like I am, you take this privilege for granted. There seems to always be something more important than reading and studying the Word of God. Somehow there are so many more exciting things to read and watch and do than to expose myself to the Scriptures. And yet there is no more important thing to do than to listen to God's voice, and study His revelation, to learn about His glorious wisdom. In fact, it is the only way we can really come to know God better—for the Bible is what tells us about God! This is why Paul later wrote to Timothy, while he was in Ephesus helping the church get established, and instructed him to devote himself "to the public reading of Scripture, to preaching and to teaching" (1 Tim. 4:13).

Yes, it is true that God reveals Himself through nature. We can see His greatness and His power. But where in nature can we learn about His love? Where can we learn about His Son who died on the cross? Where can we learn about His great plan? The Bible is the only source!

ACTION STEP

You should have two approaches to learning more about the Bible. First, you should read it regularly. Second, you should be involved in some type of in-depth Bible study—preferably in a group. Following are some questions that will help you evaluate your own life in this area:

1. Am I attending a church where the Bible is taught regularly?

NOTE: If you are not, you should!

2. Am I getting maximum benefit from the Bible teaching in my church by doing outside study on my own that correlates with the pastor's messages?

3. Do I have a Bible reading program—a program where I read portions of Scripture regularly and sequentially?

NOTE: If not, begin to read through the New Testament beginning with the gospel of John. Then when you complete the book of Revelation, read the first three gospels—Matthew, Mark, and Luke.

4. Do I have a Bible that makes reading easy?

NOTE: For this purpose *The Living Bible* is probably the best. But remember, it is only a *paraphrase*. It will not give you an accurate word-by-word translation. I personally prefer the *New International Version,* both for reading and study. And until the *New International Version Old Testament* is completed, I use the *New American Standard* for reading and studying the Old Testament.

5. Do I have a Bible that is good for study purposes?

NOTE: If you use *The Living Bible* for reading, you should definitely use a literal translation for study, such as the *New International Version.*

6. Am I attending a Bible study group or class that is designed for in-depth exposure to the Scriptures?

NOTE: If not, you may want to start one on your own. If you won't feel comfortable teaching it, search for someone who will.

FAMILY OR PERSONAL PROJECT

As the leader of your family, think seriously about what you are doing to expose your children to the Word of God. Visit your local Christian bookstore to see what Bible storybooks are available for different age levels.

As an individual Christian, if you are not involved in a regular group Bible study, take steps to become involved as soon as possible.

chapter 8
HOPE—
AND THE CHURCH
AT THESSALONICA

Maturity in a body of believers is not a constant. Neither does it always progress. In fact, in some instances a church can regress. A group of Christians that at one time manifests faith, hope and love, the true marks of maturity, can depart from its strong biblical stance.

This is pointedly illustrated by the church at Ephesus. Jesus Christ, speaking through the apostle John, charged the Ephesians, the once-dynamic and mature Ephesians, that they had gone backwards. "You have forsaken your first love." He said. "Remember the height from which you have fallen! Repent and do the things you did at first" (Rev. 2:4,5).

What a contrast! Earlier Paul had commended the Ephesians for their maturity. Now, 35 years later, they had to be reprimanded for departing from what they knew to be the will of God.

It is possible, then, to be a growing and maturing church and gradually (or even suddenly) to become confused or side-tracked. Interestingly, a church need not regress in all three aspects of maturity in order to become unstable in certain aspects of its life. What is even more subtle is the possibility of growing and developing in certain aspects of maturity and at the same time slide backwards in others.

The Thessalonian Christians graphically illustrate this phenomenon. When Paul first wrote to them he commended them for their "work produced by *faith*," their "labor prompted by *love*," and their "endurance inspired by *hope*" (1 Thess. 1:3). But when he wrote his second letter, there is a conspicuous omission in his opening paragraph—"We ought always to thank God for you, brothers, and rightly so, because your *faith is growing* more and more, and the *love* every one of you has for each other *is increasing.*" And Paul even went on to say that because of this unusual and continual development in *faith* and *love,* he was boasting about their maturity "among God's churches" (2 Thess. 1:3,4).

Note, however, that Paul said nothing about their *hope* in the second letter. And there is a reason! Someone had confused them with false doctrine.

But we're getting ahead of the story. Let's reconstruct the history of this church—without which we really can't appreciate Paul's concern in his second letter.

A CHURCH IS ESTABLISHED!

Thessalonica was a thriving commercial town located on a trade route in Macedonia. Here Paul—and his fellow missionaries, Silas and Timothy—founded the church that was destined to be one of the most talked-about churches in the New Testament world (1 Thess. 1:7,8). It was born in the midst of persecution, but gloriously thrived in spite of those who tried to destroy it (1 Thess. 1:6; 2:2,14,15). In fact, resentment and oppression became so brutal that Paul and Silas eventually had to flee the city by night because their lives were in danger (Acts 17:5,10).

But in spite of strong opposition these daring men of God won men to Christ and diligently and sensitively taught them the crucial doctrines of the Christian faith (1 Thess. 2:2-6). On the basis of the time factors mentioned in Acts 17:2, some have concluded that these New Testament evangelists were in Thessalonica only three weeks. It seems, however, it must have been a much longer period of time. True, "Paul went into the synagogue, and on three Sabbath days he reasoned with them from the Scriptures, explaining and proving that the Christ had to suffer and rise from the dead." And Luke tells us further that "some of the Jews were persuaded and joined Paul and Silas, as did a large number of the God-fearing Greeks" (Acts 17:2-4).

When all the biblical factors of this historical incident are considered, it seems that it took the first three weeks to begin to see fruit—to see men and women come to Christ. And then began the careful and exemplary process of teaching and nurturing these new believers, which Paul beautifully detailed in his first letter to the Thessalonians—"You are witnesses, and so is God, of how holy, righteous and blameless we were among you who believed. For you know that we dealt with each of you as a father deals with his own children, encouraging, comforting and urging you to live lives worthy of God" (1 Thess. 2:10-12).

During this personal process of discipling, Paul, Silas,

and Timothy did a masterful job of grounding these new believers in the major doctrines of the Christian faith. It appears he even dealt in depth with the doctrine of election, for in his first letter, Paul makes what appears to be a "passing" reference to this profound truth, demonstrating that he was simply assuming that they understood what he was talking about (1 Thess. 1:4).

But of all New Testament doctrines, it appears that Paul must have concentrated most on teaching them about the second coming of Christ. In fact, their expectancy of Christ's soon return became a hallmark of their Christian faith—"Your faith in God has become known everywhere," wrote Paul. "Therefore we do not need to say anything about it, for they themselves report what kind of reception you gave us. They tell how you turned to God from idols to serve the living and true God, and to wait for his Son from heaven, whom he raised from the dead—Jesus, who rescues us from the coming wrath" (1 Thess. 1:8-10).

Later in this same first letter, Paul implied that he had carefully gone over many details regarding the second coming of Christ when he was with them. "Now, brothers," he wrote, "about times and dates we do not need to write to you, for you know very well that the day of the Lord will come like a thief in the night" (1 Thess. 5:1). And referring to significant details that would transpire after the church is taken out of the world, Paul asked them in his second letter, "Don't you remember that when I was with you I used to tell you these things?" (2 Thess. 2:5).

Why Paul concentrated so heavily in his teaching on Christ's second coming is a matter of conjecture. But it seems quite logical to conclude that he did so because of the severe persecution these new Christians faced. The most encouraging word that Paul could give them was that they have *hope!* And that hope was the prospect of deliverance—liberation from this present evil world and translated into the eternal presence of God.

But note! What appears to be their doctrinal strength seemingly became their most vulnerable area for Satanic attack. The main ingredient that made them a model in the New Testament world (see 1 Thess. 1:7), suddenly became a point for justifiable criticism.

The enemy of our souls is a sly old rascal! If he can't hit from the front, he'll hit from behind. If coming as a roaring lion won't work, he'll try as an angel of light. And if he can't get us by attacking our weaknesses, he'll try our strengths! And that's what he did to the Thessalonians.

THE CHURCH BECOMES UNSETTLED

Uncertainty About the Rapture of the Church

Paul began his first letter by commending the Thessalonian Christians for their "endurance inspired by hope." He had received a glowing report from Timothy, who had just returned from Thessalonica after visiting them to strengthen and encourage them in their faith so that they wouldn't be unsettled by the trials they were facing (1 Thess. 3:2). He "has brought good news about your faith and love," Paul wrote with excitement (3:6).

Overall, Paul was satisfied with their spiritual progress, especially in faith and love. And overall he was pleased with their "endurance inspired by hope." At this point, they had no doubts about the fact that Jesus Christ was coming again to deliver them from their trials and tribulations.

But Timothy reported on one point of confusion, one

that had not shaken their own hope, but one that was causing some severe emotional pain. Paul spoke to that issue in his first letter. Some had no doubt misunderstood Paul's earlier teaching about the rapture of the church. They were not clear about what happens to those who die before Christ comes again. Evidently they were grieving about some Christian loved ones who had already passed on—perhaps having been martyred for Christ.

Thus Paul wrote the following, which is a very clear statement about the coming of Jesus Christ for the church and what will actually happen:

"Brothers, we do not want you to be ignorant about those who sleep, or to grieve like the rest of men, who have no hope. We believe that Jesus died and rose again and so we believe that God will bring with Jesus those who sleep in him. According to the Lord's own word, we tell you that we who are still alive, who are left till the coming of the Lord, will certainly not precede those who have fallen asleep. For the Lord himself will come down from heaven, with a loud command, with the voice of the archangel and with the trumpet call of God, and the dead in Christ will rise first. After that, we who are still alive and are left will be caught up with them in the clouds to meet the Lord in the air. And so we will be with the Lord forever. Therefore encourage each other with these words" (1 Thess. 4:13-18).

Here Paul is talking about the rapture of the church. This is the Christian's *hope!* Paul also spells this out, with some additional detail, in his first Corinthian letter: "Listen," wrote Paul, "I tell you a mystery: We shall not all sleep, but we shall all be changed—in a flash, in the twinkling of an eye, at the last trumpet. For the trumpet will sound, the dead will be raised imperishable, and we shall be changed" (1 Cor. 15:51-53).

The truth is this—not all will die! But, nevertheless, *all* will be changed when He comes—those who have died and those who are still alive. We'll *all* receive new bodies. All of those who have received Jesus Christ personally will go to live with the Lord forever.

But, somehow, in some way, the Thessalonians eventually lost this hope. And thus Paul, in the second letter, commended them for their *growing faith* and their *abounding love* (2 Thess. 1:3), but then proceeded to correct a doctrinal error that had crept into the church.

Uncertainty About the Day of the Lord

After Timothy left Thessalonica and rejoined Paul, giving him and Silas a positive report about these Christians, Satan made his attack! And he attacked one of their greatest strengths, their "endurance inspired by hope." They had withstood persecution well. They had grown in the midst of stress and oppression. They had responded to Paul's positive commendations.

But then it happened! A false prophecy, an oral report or a letter supposedly came from Paul—"saying that the day of the Lord has already come" (2 Thess. 2:1,2). Paul doesn't make clear which means Satan used, other than that it was false information and not the Word of God!

The "day of the Lord" refers not to a 24-hour day, but to a period of time. Just as we are now living in the "day of salvation" (2 Cor. 6:2) or the "day of grace," there is a period of time which is defined in Scripture as the "day of the Lord." True, it will be initiated at a particular point in time, but it will continue on for a little over a thousand years. It will be a time when God's wrath will be directly poured out on sinful men. I personally believe that the day of the Lord will include the seven-year tribulation period, the millennial reign of Christ, and will end at the great white throne judgment.

Today we're living in the day of grace. God is allowing sin, in many respects, to go unchecked. Many who are wicked are even flourishing more than those who are Christians. God "causes his sun to rise on the evil and the good, and sends rain on the righteous and the unrighteous" (Matt. 5:45). This is the "day of salvation." All men are invited to respond to the grace of God, to receive Jesus Christ as personal Saviour, and to be saved from their sins.

But a period of great judgment is coming on the earth. The Old Testament prophets spoke of it frequently (Ps. 2:9; Isa. 13:9-11; Zeph. 1:14-16), and John described it extensively and vividly in the book of Revelation. And the Thessalonians were led to believe that "that day" had already come. They were told by someone posing as Paul that they were already living in the midst of God's wrath and judgment on the earth. Paul wrote his second letter primarily to correct this false impression.

THE CHURCH IS STRENGTHENED!

Paul proceeded immediately to deal with the confusion that existed in the church at Thessalonica. He wrote: "Concerning the coming of our Lord Jesus Christ and our being gathered to him, we ask you, brothers, not to become easily unsettled or alarmed by some prophecy, report or letter supposed to have come from us, saying that the day of the Lord has already come" (2 Thess. 2:1,2).

And then Paul spelled out two major reasons why this "day" could not yet have begun. First, he told them that there would be extensive apostasy in the church (2 Thess. 2:3). This will be terrible "rebellion" against

103

God's truth—especially by those who claimed to be "followers of God!"

This, of course, correlates with Paul's words to Timothy, "Evil men and imposters will go from bad to worse, deceiving and being deceived" (2 Tim. 3:13). "For the time will come when men will not put up with sound doctrine. Instead, to suit their own desires, they will gather around them a great number of teachers to say what their itching ears want to hear. They will turn their ears away from the truth and turn aside to myths" (2 Tim. 4:3,4).

The church in the first century, generally speaking, had not yet departed from faith. There were many strong and thriving churches all over the New Testament world, churches that were manifesting faith, hope and love. Therefore, implies Paul, the day of the Lord has not yet come!

Secondly, Paul told them that this period of time would be recognized by the appearance of the "man of lawlessness" (2 Thess. 2:3)—probably the Antichrist. He could be easily recognized because he "opposes and exalts himself over everything that is called God or is worshiped, and even sets himself up in God's temple, proclaiming himself to be God" (2 Thess. 2:4).

True, there were many false Christs in this day—just as there are today. But none were performing the counterfeit miracles, signs, and wonders of evil that this man would be able to do with the power of Satan (2 Thess. 2:9,10). A Christian, of all people—if he were yet on earth—would recognize this man immediately.

It is my personal opinion that Paul's message to the Thessalonians was that Christians would not be here to witness the appearance of this "man of sin," at least in all of his sinful manifestations. In other words, the day of the Lord will begin after the church is removed from the earth. We are not destined to "suffer wrath but to receive salvation through our Lord Jesus Christ" (1 Thess. 5:9).

THE TWENTIETH-CENTURY CHURCH

There are many lessons that emerge from this study, but two stand out in bold type.

1. The church can be strong in certain areas and weak in others. This is a very subtle problem. We all tend to glory in our strengths, and to rationalize our weaknesses. This is why we need a divine standard, a measuring rod, a biblical thermometer, to constantly check our spiritual temperature.

For the church, that standard is faith, hope and love. Not one, not two, but all three! And evaluation must be *constant*, for Satan is *constantly* waiting to get his foot in the door. And one of his most deceptive tactics is to destroy balance—to get a church off kilter. He doesn't usually begin by "blowing up the building." Rather, he strikes by chipping away at the foundation and superstructure, weakening certain vital standards that cause a church to be what it should be.

Where is Satan attacking *your* church?

2. Satan often attacks a church's area of greatest strength.

The Thessalonian Christians were a model in the New Testament world. Everyone was talking about their faith, hope and love, and particularly their "endurance inspired by hope" in the midst of terrible persecution.

And at that point Satan struck. In this instance he didn't worry much about the development of their faith and love. He attacked that which was giving them stability and popularity.

What is the strongest asset in *your* church? What are people talking about? What do they like the most?

Beware!—because Satan is looking for an opportunity.

But what a privilege to have the New Testament letters, these divinely inspired manuscripts that give us examples of Satanic strategy. To be forewarned is to be forearmed. This is what God has done by giving us the Bible. We need not go down in defeat. We can be on the lookout. We can "put on the full armor of God" so that we can "stand against the devil's schemes" (Eph. 6:11). And perhaps most important for us today, we have the "sword of the Spirit, which is the word of God" (Eph. 6:17).

ACTION STEP

Evaluate your church carefully, using *faith, hope* and *love* as the measuring rod. Note your areas of greatest strength, of greatest weakness. Are your strengths related to these biblical criteria? Or are you pointing to something as a strength that is peripheral to God's standard? Maybe that false standard is growth, giving, activity, various programs, organizational efficiency, or even soul-winning or missionary interest. Remember! The true criteria are faith, hope and love—and all of these other factors must be measured in the light of these three.

FAMILY OR GROUP PROJECT

Apply this same standard to your family or small group. Review the meaning of faith, hope and love. How do you as an individual or a group measure up? What are your strengths? Your weaknesses? How do you feel Satan is attacking you? Where can you anticipate his attack?

chapter 9
FAITH—
A BIBLICAL
PERSPECTIVE

Love stands out in Scripture as the greatest mark of maturity in a local body of believers. But the words *faith* (*pistis*), and it's corollary, *belief* (*pisteuo*), appear nearly twice as many times on the pages of the New Testament as the word *love*. When combined together, the New Testament writers penned the words "faith" and "believe" nearly 500 times—about 250 each.

Obviously, this tells us something about the concept of faith—its importance and significance when describing the Christian way of life. Faith is foundational to Christianity. In fact, without it you can have no true biblical perspective. The writer to the Hebrews made this truth even more specific, and very clear: "Without faith it is impossible to please God, because anyone who comes to him must believe that he exists and that he rewards those who earnestly seek him" (Heb. 11:6).

Another reason the concept of faith appears so frequently in the New Testament is because of its varied uses and meanings. Frequently the word is used to describe "saving faith." And in the majority of instances when the word "believe" is used, it definitely refers to "saving faith."

On other occasions, the word faith is used to refer to "*the* faith," that body of content and truth that comprises Christian theology.

A third usage has to do with "the gift of faith," a special anointing by the Holy Spirit given to some—not all—within the body of Christ in the early days of the church. There is only one clear-cut reference to this gift, but there are a number of instances that seem to imply the presence of this gift in certain individuals.

And then there is a fourth usage, the one we're primarily concerned about in this book. There is "living faith," that which is visible and measurable in a local body of believers.

SAVING FAITH

That man is saved by faith, not by works, stands out as one of the most discernible doctrines in the New Testament. No truth could be more apparent than that expressed by Paul to the Ephesian Christians—"For it is by grace you have been saved, through faith—and this not from yourselves, it is the gift of God—not by works, so that no one can boast" (Eph. 2:8,9).

This truth written to the Ephesians is supported and confirmed by dozens of other scriptural statements. In fact, the major purpose behind the writing of the entire Galatian letter was to explain and clarify that salvation is a matter of faith, not works. No less than three times in the epistle, Paul asserts that a man is "justified by faith" (Gal. 2:16; 3:8,24).

The first four chapters of the Roman letter also present a careful and logical argument—using Old and New Testament examples—to demonstrate that righteousness comes "by faith" (Rom. 1:17; 3:22,28,30; 4:5,9,11, 13,22,23). And thus Paul concludes in Romans 5:1 with these words—"Therefore, since we have been justified through faith, we have peace with God through our Lord Jesus Christ."

In spite of the clarity of this Old and New Testament doctrine, every major world religion focuses on "works" as a means of salvation. And every major religious sect and "ism" that has ever broken away from the main stream of classical Christianity has as a central doctrine justification by works, not faith!

In extra-biblical church history, Martin Luther stands out as a symbol of man's struggle with this truth. Born and reared in a context that emphasized "salvation by works," he gradually and dramatically learned, from his own personal and direct study of the Scriptures, that man is saved by faith and faith alone. His discovery and his outspoken and bold propagation of this truth rocked the whole religious world, resulting in reverberations even to this very moment in history. Interestingly, since his death over 400 years ago, more books have been written about his life than any other person in history, except Jesus Christ.*

THE FAITH

The word "faith" is also used by New Testament writers to refer to a system of beliefs, a body of truths. In this sense, faith is very closely aligned with the concept of hope.

Following are some examples:

Luke records that a "large number of priests became obedient *to the faith*" (Acts 6:7).

Heretofore, many priests zealously opposed and rejected the teachings of the apostles. In fact, they had seized Peter and John and thrown them in jail. But not all religious leaders continued to resist the message that Jesus Christ was indeed the true Messiah, the Promised One who was crucified, buried, resurrected, and who ascended to the right hand of God the Father. To become "obedient to the faith" meant that they embraced the doctrines of Christianity.

By contrast, Elymas the sorcerer "tried to turn the proconsul [Sergius Paulus] *from the faith*" (Acts 13:8).

Paul and Barnabas had come to Paphos on their first missionary tour. By personal invitation they had an audience with Sergius Paulus, the governor. Luke reports that he was "an intelligent man" and "wanted to hear the word of God." But Elymas the sorcerer, one of the governor's attendants, tried to turn him away "from the faith," that is, he tried to persuade Sergius Paulus not to believe the doctrines of Christianity. As a sorcerer he knew that he would lose his job fast if the governor truly and sincerely endorsed and embraced Christianity.

"The churches were strengthened *in the faith* and grew daily in numbers" (Acts 16:5).

As Paul and Timothy left Lystra as a missionary team, they "traveled from town to town" and "delivered the decisions reached by the apostles and elders in Jerusalem for the people to obey" (Acts 16:4). In other words, they taught the people the doctrines of Christianity. Consequently, "the churches were strengthened in the faith" (16:5). That is, they were grounded in biblical truths.

"The man who formerly persecuted us is now *preaching the faith* he once tried to destroy" (Gal. 1:23).

This was written by Paul about his own conversion. Prior to his encounter with Jesus Christ on the road to Damascus, he had tried to thwart all efforts by Christians to communicate New Testament truth. But once converted, he became one of the most ardent propagators of *the Christian faith!*

"There is one body and one spirit—just as you were called to one hope when you were called—one Lord, *one faith* . . ." (Eph. 4:4).

Here Paul was writing about the basic content of the Christian faith. There is, he was saying, only *one* basic set of beliefs inherent in God's great plan of salvation for *both* Jews and Gentiles.

"Until we all reach unity *in the faith*" (Eph. 4:13).

One of the goals of Christian nurture is to produce true oneness and unity in doctrinal belief. It is then that Christians "will no longer be infants, tossed back and forth by the waves, and blown here and there by every wind of teaching . . ." (Eph. 4:14).

These, then, are but a few examples of how the word *faith* is used to refer to a basic system of theology. Others could be cited, such as in Paul's letter to Timothy. Here Paul testified that he was appointed as "a teacher of *the true faith* to the Gentiles" (1 Tim. 2:7). Later, speaking of deacons, Paul warned: "They must keep hold of the *deep truths of the faith* with a clear conscience" (3:9). And speaking of the last days, Paul cautioned that "some will *abandon the faith*" (4:1).

THE GIFT OF FAITH

In the early days of the church God definitely endowed certain members of the body of Christ with the *gift of faith.* Interestingly, this special gift of the Spirit was not necessarily related to spiritual maturity. On the one hand some of the Corinthians possessed this gift and were a hindrance to the gospel. On the other hand, mature men like Stephen, Barnabas, and Timothy may have also had this special gift (Acts 6:5; 11:24; 2 Tim. 1:5-7) and were greatly used by God to further the word of Christ.

It seems that the possession of spiritual gifts and spiritual maturity were not necessarily synonymous. The Holy Spirit obviously gave gifts to babes in Christ, and if these new Christians did not grow spiritually, they did not necessarily lose their gifts (1 Cor. 1:4-6; 3:1-3).

LIVING FAITH

"Saving faith" is intensely personal. It produces individual conversion, and is that means whereby a person becomes a member of the body of Jesus Christ. When the Bible refers to "the faith" it is referring to that body of truth that makes up our Christian theology. The "gift of faith" seems to have been a special gift that God gave to certain Christians in the early days of the church to help Christians grow and mature in *the* Christian *faith.* But *living faith* is ongoing and reflects maturity in a local body of believers. Actually, it is the continuation and development of *saving faith.* This is the kind of faith that Paul was referring to when he said to the Corinthians, "And now these three remain: *faith,* hope and love" (1 Cor. 13:13).

This kind of faith is both individual and corporate.

This is also true, of course, of both *hope* and *love.* Christianity is intensely personal. A demonstration of "corporate hope" must be based on "personal hope" among individual Christians. "Corporate love" obviously reflects the results of each Christian in a local body expressing love. Likewise with faith! "Corporate faith" reflects the faith of individual Christians.

Though faith *is* personal, even living faith, we must take note of the fact that the majority of references in the New Testament letters refers to "corporate faith." When Paul greeted the believers in Rome, Ephesus, Colosse, and Thessalonica—he thanked God for *their* faith, that is, *their* faith as a body! (See Rom. 1:8; Eph. 1:15; Col. 1:4; 1 Thess. 1:3; 2 Thess. 1:3.)

In all of these references Paul is referring to corporate faith. The exciting thing about this truth is that individual Christians, who are weak in faith and immature in their Christian lives, can also be "a part" of a body that generally reflects a strong and vibrant faith! And to be a part of this kind of body develops the personal faith of those who may be weak. The very exposure to other members of the body will cause them to grow spiritually. To see God answer prayer as a result of corporate faith will encourage them to exercise their own personal faith in Jesus Christ.

This kind of faith is observable.

When Paul wrote to the Roman Christians he said, "First, I thank my God through Jesus Christ for all of you, because *your faith* is being reported *all over the* world" (Rom. 1:8). And to the Thessalonian Christians, he said, "Your *faith in God* has become known *everywhere*" (1 Thess. 1:8).

Herein lies the uniqueness of the body of Christ. True, personal faith can and should be observable. But body function is a much more dynamic process. Faith, when expressed through a "body" of Christians, has a power of expression and a visibility that is nearly impossible to match by a Christian who is living out his faith in isolation.

The same is true, of course, with *hope* and *love*. God's primary plan is to reveal these three virtues to others via the "group process," via the body that "builds itself up in love, as each part does its work" (Eph. 4:16).

This kind of faith can and should grow.

Paul's second letter to the Thessalonians makes this point very clear. "We ought always to thank God for you, brothers, and rightly so", he wrote. And why was Paul thankful? Because "your faith is *growing* more and more" (2 Thess. 1:3).

Here was a New Testament church whose faith was being talked about everywhere, even at the time Paul wrote his first letter. But later, after he had received a good report from Timothy, he was rejoicing that the dynamic faith that had already been observable to the whole community was growing even more.

"Living faith," both in individual Christians and in a body, must never be static. If it is, it will more often than not be in a state of deterioration. A mature church never stands still—in faith, hope, or love! If it does, something is wrong with the growth process itself.

This kind of faith is foundational to becoming a mature body.

When Paul and Silas had to leave Thessalonica to escape from those who wanted to kill them, they continued to be very concerned about the new believers they had left behind to face the ongoing persecution. Paul was fearful that someone might sidetrack them and discourage them in their Christian lives. Thus Paul wrote in his first letter:

"We sent Timothy . . . to strengthen and encourage you *in your faith,* so that no one would be unsettled by these trials. . . . For this reason . . . I sent to find out about *your faith.* . . . But Timothy has just now come to us from you and has brought good news about *your faith*. . . . Therefore, brothers, in all our distress and persecution we were encouraged about you because of *your faith*. . . . Night and day we pray most earnestly that we may see you again and supply what is lacking in *your faith*" (1 Thess. 3:1-3,5-7,10).

Within the space of one chapter Paul mentioned five times his concern about the faith of these new believers. He knew that if they failed at this level, they would not go on and develop the other qualities of maturity—hope and love. Thus he was overjoyed with Timothy's report—so much so that he wrote: "For now we really live, since you are standing firm in the Lord" (1 Thess. 3:8).

This kind of faith defeats Satan.

The Ephesian Christians faced some unusual struggles with demonic influence and activity. Many of these Christians had been delivered from occult practices. In fact, a number of those converted to Christ in this city "who had practiced sorcery brought their scrolls together and burned them publicly. When they calculated the value of the scrolls, the total came to 50,000 drachmas" (Acts 19:19). (A drachma was about a day's wage.)

Satan and his evil cohorts do not easily go down in defeat. And no doubt they continued to harass some of these New Testament Christians. Consequently, Paul exhorted them to "take up the shield of faith" with which they could "extinguish all the flaming arrows of the evil one" (Eph. 6:16). Faith, then, is a special key that unlocks the power of God against Satan.

THE TWENTIETH-CENTURY CHURCH

In many parts of the world today, particularly in our Western culture, it is difficult for many believers to identify with the concept of faith. "Saving faith"—yes! We've experienced salvation. *"The* faith"—yes again! Because most of us know what we believe. In fact, the New Testament with its glorious body of truth is a special gift to us that was not available to first-century Christians. The special "gift of faith" is probably no longer in existence, though some will disagree with me at this point.

It is "living faith" that is frequently difficult for twentieth-century Christians to identify with! Why is this true?

Suppose that we awakened tomorrow morning and all references in the Bible to "living" and "walking by faith" were missing. Would it really make any difference in our lives? Or would we be able to go right on in our Christian lives as if nothing had happened? We still had a job. We still had a little money in the bank. We still had a home that was ours—as long as we made the payments. Our late model cars were still in good running condition. And even though gas was expensive, we could still fill up a couple of times a week. The supermarkets were stocked with food, and "McDonald's" was just a block or two away. Most of us still had good relationships with our neighbors, and even those who practice non-Christian religions left us alone.

In other words, why, as twentieth-century Christians living in today's world, do we need to "live by faith"?

On the other hand, what would be our attitude if suddenly our jobs were taken away, our bank accounts confiscated, our homes destroyed, our means of transportation eliminated, our food supply removed, and we began to suffer extensive persecution from those who hate Christianity? If we can identify with this kind of crisis, we can then identify with many New Testament Christians. We can begin to understand, at least vicariously, why many *had* to live by faith! We can also identify with Paul's concern that the Thessalonians and Philippians and other New Testament Christians, who were in the midst of tremendous persecution, might become unsettled in their faith.

ACTION STEP

But what does all of this say to *us*—especially those of us who are not suffering these things—at least not yet! Should we feel guilty and ashamed because of our great blessings? No! We should rejoice in everything God has given us. But we should feel guilty and ashamed when we complain and nag and get upset with God when the dishwasher breaks down, when our power boat motor won't start in the spring, when we have to tighten our budgets a little because of inflation—causing us to have to eat at McDonald's rather than at the local steak house.

As an individual Christian and as a body of believers, evaluate your attitude toward the Christian life. How strong is your faith? Are you a Christian because it's convenient and you've never really had to live by faith? One good test of the depth of our Christian experience is how we act—right now—when we really don't have to "live by faith."

Here is a good passage of Scripture to meditate on, to memorize, to put into practice: "Continue to work out your salvation with fear and trembling, for it is God who works in you to will and to act according to his good purpose. Do everything without complaining or arguing, so that you may become blameless and pure, children of God without fault in a crooked and depraved generation, in which you shine like stars in the universe as you hold out the word of life" (Phil. 2:12-16).

FAMILY OR GROUP PROJECT

Spend time reviewing these concepts and then thank God for our tremendous blessings that most of us have who live in the twentieth-century culture. Confess any attitudes and acts of unthankfulness.

NOTE: If you are truly having difficulties in your Christian life, if your needs are not being met, if your trials are really more than you can bear—then perhaps the next two chapters will be an encouragement to you because we want to see what New Testament Christians did in the midst of "trials" that were *really* "trials"!

The New International Dictionary of the Christian Church (Grand Rapids: Zondervan, 1974), p. 611.

chapter 10

FAITH— AND THE HEBREW CHRISTIANS

The Bible is a marvelous book of illustrations—illustrations that can help us become mature in Christ, both as individuals and as a body of believers. We've looked at the church at Corinth, at Ephesus, at Thessalonica, at Colosse, at Rome, at Philippi, and at the churches scattered throughout the province of Galatia. All of these groups of New Testament believers have taught us dramatic lessons about maturity—and immaturity. All have given us authoritative guidelines for measuring ourselves as a local church.

But we want to look at still another church, or perhaps a group of churches in the New Testament; Christians we know about because of the New Testament correspondence identified as the "Epistle to the Hebrews."

This letter was written to a body of believers who were yet immature. Though they were completed Jews,

God's chosen people who had truly believed in their Messiah, they still had much to learn about the Christian life. The author (some believe it was Paul, but we do not know for sure) spoke very directly to their problem, almost as pointedly as Paul spoke to the Corinthians about their immaturity: "You are slow to learn," he wrote. "In fact, though by this time you ought to be teachers, you need someone to teach you the elementary truths of God's word all over again. You need milk, not solid food! Anyone who lives on milk, being still an infant, is not acquainted with the teaching about righteousness. But solid food is for the mature, who by constant use have trained themselves to distinguish good from evil" (Heb. 5:11-14).

And then the author of this Hebrew letter drove home a very important point of major concern in writing this epistle: "Therefore let us leave the elementary teachings about Christ and go on to maturity" (6:1).

After careful explanation in the first part of the letter that Christ is the great high priest and the one, final and perfect sacrifice for sins, the author, interestingly but not surprisingly, went on to spell out the true criteria for measuring maturity in a body of believers. Note what he wrote:

First, "Let us draw near to God with a sincere heart in full assurance of *faith*" (10:22).

Second, "Let us hold unswervingly to the *hope* we profess, for he who promised is faithful" (10:23).

Third, "Let us consider how we may spur one another on toward *love* and good deeds" (10:24).

Here it is again—the criteria for maturity in a body of believers—*faith, hope* and *love!* These are indeed the marks of a mature church.

But the author's concern in this epistle now zeroes

in on one basic ingredient—FAITH. Let's look carefully at what he wrote.

AN EXHORTATION TO FAITH

A developing and expanding faith is foundational to spiritual growth in a church. Without it, hope and love cannot grow effectively.

The Hebrew Christians, like so many other New Testament Christians, were facing intensive persecution. Previously, they had stood their ground "in the face of suffering." When "publicly exposed to insult and persecution" they had accepted it with a positive attitude. They had "sympathized with those in prisons" and had "joyfully accepted the confiscation" of their property (10:32-34).

Their motivation? They knew that all these things were temporal, including this life itself, and that beyond death were eternal possessions (10:34).

Consequently, these Christians were exhorted not to change now but to keep on for Jesus Christ; not to "throw away [their] confidence," but to persevere in doing the will of God. In short, they were exhorted to continue to "live by faith" and not to "shrink back" in unbelief (10:35-39).

Living by faith is not automatic. It includes human responsibility. Twice Paul told Timothy to "pursue . . . faith" (1 Tim. 6:11; 2 Tim. 2:22). And Paul wrote to the Thessalonian Christians that he was praying night and day so that he might come and supply what was "lacking in [their] faith" (1 Thess. 3:10).

Thus the church that is manifesting faith as a mark of maturity must give special attention to this virtue. Faith will not grow in a vacuum. Even faith that is saving faith "comes from hearing the message, and the message is heard through the word of Christ" (Rom. 10:17).

But what is faith, particularly as a mark of maturity in a local body of believers?

A DEFINITION OF FAITH

The Hebrew writer follows his *exhortation to faith* with a succinct *definition of faith:* "Now faith is being sure of what we hope for and certain of what we do not see" (11:1).

Out of context it is difficult to get the full meaning of this definition. On the surface it may appear that God is asking the impossible; that He is catering to the non-intellectual, to the gullible; that He is asking for faith without facts! God has never operated that way. It is against His nature. The fact is, there are numerous facts! The problem is man himself, for he refuses to look at them. But let's look more carefully at what is meant by Hebrews 11:1.

First, faith is "being sure" of something.

As we've seen, the author of this letter leads up to this definition by using such synonyms as having "confidence" (10:35), by giving an exhortation to "persevere" and not to "shrink back" (10:36,38). And in Hebrews 11:1, he uses still another synonym—to be "certain."

Second, this faith—which reflects being sure, having confidence, perseverance, and certainty—involves something "we do not see."

This, of course, is a difficult concept for many people to accept, primarily because they don't understand what is being said. "I won't believe in anything I cannot see," they say. They don't realize, of course, that what they are saying is not true. In fact, their statement is absurd because everyone—even those who claim to be agnostics and atheists—believe many things they cannot see. For example, we cannot see radio waves, and yet anyone who listens to a radio or watches television believes these invisible phenomena exist. We cannot see these waves, but through the miracle of science and electronics we see the evidence of their existence.

Neither can we see magnetic forces, but we know they exist by what we see attracted to them. Likewise, we cannot see the force of gravity, but every time we board a "jumbo jet" we put our faith in its existence. If these forces were not a reality, these monstrous machines could never navigate.

Furthermore, we cannot see ultraviolet light or infrared light. Yet we know these phenomena also exist because we can see the results of their presence.

And perhaps one of the most intriguing realities to scientists are neutrinos, tiny particles that constantly bombard the earth, passing right through it and actually passing right through *us*. We can't see them, we can't feel them, and we don't know anything about their reason for existence. But they are there. We know they are there because scientists have been able to isolate their existence through sophisticated processes that are even difficult to explain.

The same principle we've been illustrating from science is true in the spiritual realm. To have faith, to be "sure of what we hope for and certain of what we do not see" is not "a leap in the dark." The non-Christian existentialist may define faith in this way, but not the Bible. Biblical faith is an *intelligent* faith, a *rational* faith, a faith rooted in the facts of history.

That which "we do not see" is very clearly defined in the book of Hebrews in two ways. The first aspect of that which "we do not see" is in the contrast between the two priesthoods.

The first priesthood was temporal; the second is eternal. One involved mere man; the second, the God-man. One was an Old Testament concept; the second a New Testament concept. And perhaps most significantly, the former was *visible;* the latter *invisible.*

In Old Testament days the children of Israel could *see* the high priest as he went about his religious duties. They could *see* him cleanse himself. They could *see* him offer sacrifices for himself and for the nation. They could *see* the very process of atonement taking place, again and again. And they were taught to fear the way they approached God since He dwelt in the holy of holies in the earthly Tabernacle. And rightly so, for God is a holy God to be revered and honored.

But the message of the Hebrew letter presents an eternal high priest—Jesus Christ, who "appeared once for all at the end of the ages to do away with sin by the sacrifice of himself" (Heb. 9:26). He then arose from the dead, ascended into glory, *disappeared from sight* (Acts 1:9), and then "sat down at the right hand of the Majesty in heaven" (Heb. 1:3).

This High Priest, of course, was no longer visible to these New Testament Christians, nor is He to us. But, writes this author, He *is* a reality just the same. Though we cannot see Him, He exists. And because He "lives forever, he has a permanent priesthood. Therefore he is able to save completely those who come to God through him, because he always lives to intercede for them" (7:24,25). The message, then, is this: "since we have a great high priest over the house of God, let us draw near to God with a sincere heart in full assurance of faith" (10:21; see also 4:14-16).

In other words, what a Christian cannot see, but yet can be sure of, is Jesus Christ and that He exists as the eternal High Priest in heaven. And that kind of faith is not blind faith—but faith that is rooted in historical fact (1 Cor. 15:3-8).

The second aspect of what "we do not see" relates to heaven itself. The author of Hebrews writes of an "eternal city" where we shall eventually live with Christ forever. That the author is referring to heaven as a real but now unseen place is dramatically illustrated in his references to the Old Testament saints. After writing about Abel, Enoch, Noah, and Abraham, we read:

"All these people were still living by faith when they died. They did not receive the things promised; they only saw them and welcomed them from a distance. And they admitted that they were foreigners and strangers on earth. People who say such things show that they are looking for a country of their own. If they had been thinking of the country they had left, they would have had opportunity to return. Instead, they were longing for a better country—a heavenly one. Therefore, God is not ashamed to be called their God, for he has prepared a city for them" (Heb. 11:13-16).

The fact is, of course, that God has not chosen to reveal the location or supply a literal description of heaven to His creatures. However, just as God has allowed scientists to demonstrate that magnetic and gravitational forces do indeed exist, so He has given the world plenty of evidence that heaven is an eternal reality. He has done many unusual things to give us facts on which to build our faith.

The most dramatic thing God did, of course, was to send His Son into this world to tell us that heaven is an eternal reality. While walking this earth and working many miracles, Jesus said one day to His disciples: "Do not let your hearts be troubled. *Trust* [have faith] in God;

trust [have faith] also in me. There are many rooms in my Father's house; otherwise, I would have told you. I am going there to prepare a place for you, I will come back and take you to be with me that you also may be where I am" (John 14:1-3).

These two concepts, then, comprise the essence of the Hebrew letter. *Faith in these realities* is certainly a primary concern of the Hebrew author; but he is just as concerned about *the fact upon which our faith in these realities rests.* And this is the historical evidence that Jesus Christ was a real person who came into this world, who taught the truth, and who truly demonstrated the glory of God. This is one reason why the author of this letter began his correspondence with these words:

"In the past God spoke to our forefathers through the prophets at many times and in various ways, but in these last days he has spoken to us by his Son, whom he appointed heir of all things, and through whom he made the universe. The Son is the radiance of God's glory and the exact representation of his being, sustaining all things by his powerful word. After he had provided purification for sins, he sat down at the right hand of the Majesty in heaven" (Heb. 1:1-3).

Space prohibits a lengthy development of all that is implied in these powerful words. In essence, this brief but profound paragraph summarizes all that God has done to communicate to man, not only that He exists, but also what man needs to know and to do to inherit eternal life. Suffice it to say, God constantly revealed Himself in the Old Testament, through revelatory dreams and visions, saying the same thing to many different people over a period of many years. In addition He thundered from Sinai, actually speaking in words man could hear and understand (Exod. 19:10-25; 20:1-21).

The grand culmination of communication was when His miracle-working Son came to earth to radiate God's glory and power—the very power that made the universe. And again God did not do this in secret. We read: "This salvation, which was first announced by the Lord, was confirmed to us by those who heard him. God also testified to it by signs, wonders and various miracles, and gifts of the Holy Spirit distributed according to his will" (Heb. 2:3,4).

But how do we know these things are true?

There are those, of course, who still will not believe. One of their great and final arguments centers around the reliability of the Scriptures which records this information. "How do we know that these are real facts?" they ask. May I first of all remind you that history generally bears outstanding witness to the fact that Jesus Christ existed. Then, too, the very calendar which we use in the majority of the world is based on Christ's existence. History is broken down into two categories, B.C. (before Christ) and A.D. (after Christ's birth—literally, anno Domini). This would be a strange phenomenon indeed if Christ were merely a myth or even just an ordinary man.

But what about the Bible?

How do we know the Scriptures were really inspired by God and are accurate in their facts? Actually the Bible itself bears witness in many ways to its accuracy and reliability. The way it is authored, its fulfilled prophecies, its verification through recent archaeological discoveries, its supra-cultural relevance—all these things point to supernatural guidance in its composition and preservation. When a person really becomes aware of its origin, its content, and its uniqueness, it actually takes more faith to believe this Book is purely human in its origins than to believe it is divinely inspired. In fact, many people who criticize the Bible and do not believe it is accurate have had very little exposure to its actual history and content. Many times their statements are based upon very superficial judgments. Anyone who has studied the Bible carefully cannot but recognize its supernatural dimensions, even a non-Christian.

Christian faith, then, can be based on more than ignorance or unsupported speculations. Jesus Christ and heaven are realities that God has revealed to us in many ways. And though we cannot now literally see our great High Priest and the place He now abides, we can see with the eye of faith, just as many people have done throughout history. And the fact also remains that some-day "every eye will see him, even those who pierced him" (Rev. 1:7).

THE TWENTIETH-CENTURY CHURCH

One of the great criticisms of the church throughout history, but also in this present century, is that as Christians we've often been naive and anti-intellectual. We have not been doing our homework! Often we're not prepared to face the criticisms of the world! Our children grow up with questions we can't answer because we haven't kept up with the efforts of the secular community.

Unfortunately, many churches are not answering the questions young people are asking. In fact, some youth are afraid to ask questions for fear of rejection, or in some instances, they don't want to hurt their pastor or parents.

Often, combined with this mentality is inconsistent Christian living—a lack of Christlikeness—in short, a lack of love in the body, whether in the church or the family unit.

128

This combination is devastating to faith. It destroys, disillusions, and often leads to despair.

If we ever have to make a choice, it's far better to *live* Christlike, than to have all the answers and violate what we believe with our lives. If we do the latter, frequently people will reject what we've taught them—accurate though it may be—because we have not *verified the reality* of our theological system by backing it up with our *life-style*.

I grew up in a church that was, I'm sure, a very extreme example of this kind of mentality. They were even anti-education. When I joined the church I almost dropped out of high school because I was taught that Christians don't need an education. Somehow the Holy Spirit was supposed to teach me everything I needed to know.

Fortunately, I eventually saw through this extreme isolationism and left the movement. But the general effects of it marked my life for some time. Because of this extremely narrow exposure, I had a terrible period of frustration in college. For the first time in my life I was severely challenged in my faith. I had no real answers. Why was I a Christian and not something else? I didn't really know!

There was a second factor, however, that combined with the first to make me extremely vulnerable to Satan's attacks in my life. Not only were my theological foundations weakened still further in college, but after leaving the religious group I grew up in, I committed myself to a body of believers who, though theologically sound, did not live consistent Christian lives, particularly in relationship to one another. There was backbiting, mistrust, and certainly little love—particularly among some of the leaders of the church.

This was a crowning blow to my faith! I believe I

could have withstood the attacks in college, but the lack of love in the church was the crowning blow. I nearly crumbled. In fact, there were times when I thought I would never recover from my disillusionment. I couldn't pray! I couldn't read my Bible! I lost my motivation for living! I felt life was futile with nothing to live for!

Fortunately, God used a series of circumstances to change my life—and He did it by rebuilding my faith through people, through Christians who both gave me answers to my theological questions and demonstrated Jesus Christ in their lives.

And now I look back at those experiences as very strengthening and helpful. But I hesitate to think what would have happened to my life if I had not met true, honest, and sincere Christians who helped restore my faith. I thank God for them!

ACTION STEP

May it never be said of your church or my church that we have destroyed faith rather than built it. Following are the three exhortations the author of the Hebrew letter set before New Testament Christians. How would you evaluate your church?

1. "Let us draw near to God with a sincere heart in full assurance of faith, having our hearts sprinkled to cleanse us from guilty conscience and having our bodies washed with pure water" (10:22).

Unsatisfactory   1   2   3   4   5   Satisfactory

2. "Let us hold unswervingly to the hope we profess, for he who promised is faithful" (10:23).

Unsatisfactory   1   2   3   4   5   Satisfactory

3. "And let us consider how we may spur one another

on toward love and good deeds. Let us not give up meeting together, as some are in the habit of doing, but let us encourage one another—and all the more as you see the Day approaching" (10:24,25).

Unsatisfactory   1   2   3   4   5   Satisfactory

FAMILY OR GROUP PROJECT

What are you doing as parents to develop the faith of your children? Remember there are two ingredients—adequate answers to deep questions, and consistent Christian living that demonstrates the reality of the Christian faith. Encourage your children to ask questions that are bothering them, and to express any disillusionments they might have about the pattern of living in your home. If you approach this assignment prayerfully and carefully, it could change the direction of your family life.

NOTE: You may not have all the answers to their questions. Don't let that frustrate you. No one does! Admit you don't, but assure them you'll find out from someone what the answers really are! Children and youth are very sympathetic to "honesty," but very threatened by someone who tries to "fake it."

chapter 11
FAITH—
HOW IT CAN
BE RECOGNIZED

Faith, like hope and love, should be visible in a local body of believers. When it is, it reflects maturity.

As stated previously, personal faith can and should be observable. But body function is a much more dynamic process. Faith, when expressed through a body of Christians, has a power of expression and a visibility that is impossible to match by a single Christian who is living out his faith by himself in the midst of the world.

How, then, can it be recognized? When is faith an expression of Christian maturity?

FAITH IS VISIBLE THROUGH WORSHIP

The concept of expressing faith (as well as hope and love) through the *body* of Christ is very clear in the epistle to the Hebrews. Though personal illustrations involving Old Testament saints are used to support the injunction to "live by faith" (Abraham, Isaac, Jacob, Joseph, Moses, etc.), yet there is a decided shift to a corporate expression of faith when the author talks about the church. Thus he wrote: "Let *us* draw near to God with a sincere heart in full assurance of faith" (Heb. 10:22).

Note the "body emphasis" in the following series of "let us" injunctions:

1. Let *us* draw near to God . . . in full assurance of faith (10:22);
2. Let *us* hold unswervingly to the hope (10:23);
3. Let *us* consider how we may spur one another on toward love (10:24);
4. Let *us* not give up meeting together (10:25);
5. Let *us* encourage one another (10:25);
6. Let *us* throw off everything that hinders (12:1);
7. Let *us* run with perseverance (12:1);
8. Let *us* fix our eyes on Jesus (12:2).

Christians who are "living by faith" and expressing that faith approach God without fear. They *know* that they have been cleansed from sin by the blood of Jesus Christ.

In Old Testament days, the children of Israel could approach God only if they had engaged in various ceremonial cleansings and sacrifices. Time after time they would have to participate in these rituals. But when Jesus Christ came to earth, He was "the Lamb of God, who takes away the sin of the world" (John 1:29). And when He died on the cross, He "offered for all time one sacrifice for sins." And when He ascended to heaven, He "sat down at the right hand of God" (Heb. 10:12). Jesus is our mediator and great high priest. Paul dramatically emphasized this truth when he wrote to Timothy: "For there is one God and one mediator between God and men, the man Christ Jesus, who gave himself as a ransom for all men" (1 Tim. 2:5).

This glorious reality should affect the way Christians worship. There is no need to engage in ritualistic behavior *in order* to become acceptable to God. We can come directly into His presence—reverently, yes, but without fear. We need no human priest, no minister, no other human agent to lead us to God. Jesus Christ is our Priest, our Shepherd, our great Master. Any other person within a local body of Christ is definitely *one* member of the body. Even those who are leaders are but members of the body. These men are certainly responsible for a greater share of teaching, shepherding, and managing the flock of God, but they in no way have greater access to God, nor do they represent the means by which other members of the body of Christ approach God. We are *one* in the Spirit, *one* in the Lord, and "one in heart and mind" (Acts 4:32). And together, as one body, we are to "draw near to God with a sincere heart in full assurance of faith" (Heb. 10:22).

This kind of worship is visible and recognizable—and powerful. It affects both Christians and non-Christians. Mature Christians are made more mature. Weak Christians are made strong. And non-Christians—when they see it and experience it—cannot ignore the impact of this kind of witness. In their own hearts looms that eternal longing to know God too, and to find their rest in Him.

FAITH IS VISIBLE THROUGH PERSEVERANCE

Again the letter to the Hebrew Christians becomes our example for learning how to visibly express faith. Following the great faith chapter with its dynamic Old Testament illustrations, the author, like a coach working with a select group of sprinters, spells out the ground rules for manifesting faith: "Let us [as a body] throw off everything that hinders and the sin that so easily entangles, and let us run with perseverance the race marked out for us. Let us fix our eyes on Jesus, the

Pioneer and Perfecter of our faith, who for the joy set before him endured the cross, scorning its shame, and sat down at the right hand of the throne of God" (Heb. 12:1,2).

The author of Hebrews presents two lessons a body of believers can learn from these Old Testament saints.

We Must Be as Unencumbered as Possible

Let us throw off everything that hinders and the sin that so easily entangles (12:1).

Faith can only be expressed effectively through a local body of believers as we lay aside everything that would keep us from reaching the goal of Christian maturity. Coming right to the point, the author is talking about sin. And to make the point even more clear he spells out in the rest of his letter exactly what that sin consists of—bitterness, immorality, materialism and legalism.

Make every effort to live in peace with all men and to be holy; without holiness no one will see the Lord. See to it that no one misses the grace of God and that no bitter root grows up to cause trouble and defile many (Heb. 12:14,15).

Bitterness has a withering effect on a body of believers. It destroys faith rather than builds it. When Christians get their eyes on each others' faults rather than on the perfection of Jesus Christ, there is only one result—distrust and disillusionment. Again and again the Scriptures admonish Christians to "make every effort to keep the unity of the Spirit through the bond of peace" (Eph. 4:3).

See that no one is sexually immoral. . . . Marriage should be honored by all, and the marriage bed kept pure, for God will judge the adulterer and all the sexually immoral (Heb. 12:16; 13:4).

Immorality and Christianity are incompatible. This,

135

of course, creates an unusual tension between Christianity and our contemporary culture. The world today, even in America where our philosophy governing human relationships has been built upon the Hebrew-Christian tradition, ignores the value system of the Bible. Consequently, even some Christians have begun to question the high standards of Scripture that govern sexual behavior.

In the New Testament world, immorality was the norm. But wherever the Christian message was proclaimed, a new value system was taught—a value system emphasizing sexual purity. Sex was for marriage. Within this God-ordained relationship it was good, beautiful, and proper. In fact, not to engage in sex in marriage was a sin, both against God and the other marriage partner (1 Cor. 7:1-7). But outside of marriage sexual expression is sin.

Immorality, like bitterness, destroys faith rather than builds it. Because of its guilt-producing effects it certainly militates against drawing "near to God with a sincere heart in full assurance of faith, having our hearts sprinkled to cleanse us from a guilty conscience" (Heb. 10:22).

Keep your lives free from the love of money and be content with what you have, because God has said, "Never will I leave you; never will I forsake you." So we say with confidence, "The Lord is my helper; I will not be afraid. What can man do to me?" (Heb. 13:5,6).

Don't misunderstand! The Bible does not teach that we are to be "free from money" but rather we are to be free from the *love* of money—materialism. It does not even teach that it is wrong to accumulate money—unless our motive is to substitute material things for our dependence on God.

This is the truth of this passage. The Hebrew author is saying the same thing that Jesus said: "You cannot

136

serve both God and money" (Matt. 6:24). Rather, we are to "seek first his kingdom and his righteousness, and all of these things will be given to you as well" (Matt. 6:33).

A materialistically minded group of Christians certainly are not demonstrating and building faith. Rather, their behavior is earthly-oriented and self-centered. They are placing their faith in what "they can see" rather than in what "they cannot see."

Do not be carried away by all kinds of strange teachings. It is good for our hearts to be strengthened by grace, not by ceremonial foods, which are of no value to those who eat them (Heb. 13:9).

The Hebrew Christians were lapsing into legalism. They were reverting to old patterns and practices, doing things to make themselves righteous—in this case, partaking of "ceremonial foods." This, of course, worked against the concept of faith.

The Galatian Christians had a similar problem, though the issue among them was circumcision. Thus Paul spoke pointedly to them, contrasting faith and works: "Mark my words! I, Paul, tell you that if you let yourselves be circumcised, Christ will be of no value to you at all. Again I declare to every man who lets himself be circumcised that he is obligated to obey the whole law. You who are trying to be justified by law have been alienated from Christ; you have fallen away from grace. But by faith we eagerly await through the Spirit the righteousness for which we hope. For in Christ Jesus neither circumcision nor uncircumcision has any value. The only thing that counts is faith expressing itself through love" (Gal. 5:2-6).

Legalistic attitudes among Christians also destroy faith rather than build it. We tend to get our eyes off of Jesus

Christ and on to those things we are doing or not doing to make ourselves righteous. Legalism breeds pride and judgmental attitudes and behavior.

We Must Keep Our Eyes on the Goal

Let us fix our eyes on Jesus, the Pioneer and Perfecter of our faith (Heb. 12:2).

A foot-runner must look straight ahead! If he becomes involved with the circumstances surrounding him, his opponents or the "cheering" or "jeering" crowds, he is in danger of falling behind.

Christians who demonstrate a strong and dynamic faith must also keep their eyes on their goal which is to become like Jesus Christ. He is our great example. He pioneered in this race and won it. He went before us. He can identify with every problem we face—fear, weariness, pride, and every temptation. He became like us "in order that he might become a merciful and faithful high priest. . . . Because he himself suffered when he was tempted, he is able to help those who are being tempted" (Heb. 2:17,18).

Jesus Christ, of course, paid the supreme sacrifice in His struggle against sin. He "endured the cross, scorning its shame" (Heb. 12:2). And then the Hebrews writer reminded these New Testament Christians that in *their* "struggle against sin," they had "not yet resisted to the point of shedding [their] blood" (Heb. 12:4).

Jesus went all the way. He was the perfect example of "faith in action." He *knew* what lay beyond death and the grave. *And by faith* He faced His opposition without flinching.

FAITH IS VISIBLE THROUGH WORKS

Many sincere and well-meaning people have become

thoroughly confused about the relationship between faith and works in the Christian life. And there *is* a relationship. When Paul wrote to the Thessalonian Christians, he thanked God for their "work produced by faith" (1 Thess. 1:3). And James wrote that "faith by itself, if it is not accompanied by action, is dead" (Jas. 2:17).

What exactly *is* the relationship between faith and works? The answer is really quite simple and very clear in the Word of God. For example, Paul wrote to the Ephesians that "by grace you have been saved, through faith—and this not from yourselves, it is the gift of God—not by works, so that no one can boast." But, continued Paul, "we are God's workmanship, created in Christ Jesus to do good works, which God prepared in advance for us to do" (Eph. 2:8-10).

You see, salvation results from faith—faith in Christ's finished work. But faith that is truly faith—faith that is saving faith—will produce works. If it does not, it is no doubt a "dead faith," a faith that does not produce salvation.

James reminds us that it is not enough to believe in God. "Even the demons believe that—and shudder" (Jas. 2:19). Saving faith produces good deeds—deeds of kindness and love.

How is faith expressed through works? There are many ways, but one of the most obvious manifestations of faith in the New Testament was sacrificial concern for fellow believers through sharing material possessions. The Thessalonians, whom Paul commended for their "work of faith," were no doubt among those in Macedonia who shared with others out of "extreme poverty." Paul, writing to the Corinthians, testified "they gave as much as they were able, and even beyond their ability" (2 Cor. 8:3). This was truly a "work of faith."

139

The Philippians (Macedonians) shared in this type of sacrificial service too. Many of them gave to help Paul when they really had nothing to give. Speaking of their gifts, Paul referred to them as "a fragrant offering, an acceptable sacrifice, pleasing to God" (Phil. 4:18). Earlier he made this comment about their gift: "But even if I am being poured out like a drink offering on the sacrifice and service coming from your faith, I am glad and rejoice with all of you" (Phil. 2:17).

James, too, when writing about the relationship between faith and works, explained this relationship with a similar illustration: "What good is it, my brothers, if a man claims to have faith but has no deeds? Can such faith save him? Suppose a brother or sister is without clothes and daily food. If one of you says to him, 'Go, I wish you well; keep warm and well fed,' but does nothing about his physical needs, what good is it? In the same way, faith by itself, if it is not accompanied by action, is dead" (Jas. 2:14-17).

Again, James is not saying that works bring salvation. Rather, he is saying that true faith reveals itself in good deeds. And one of the real marks of true faith is being willing to share one's material blessings with those who have physical needs—especially when we're giving that which we really need ourselves. And New Testament Christians that were mature Christians demonstrated their faith in this way.

THE TWENTIETH-CENTURY CHURCH

Many churches today, when measured by these reflections of faith, seem to fall short. Take *worship*. Frequently what is called a "worship service" is cold and nonpersonal, even in some of our churches that pride themselves on teaching the Bible. It is often quite void of feeling, personal relationships, and focus on human needs. Singing, praying, and Scripture reading seem to be taking place in a meaningless vacuum. Members of the body often seem to be uninvolved, while the pastor, choir members, and perhaps a few other people, "perform."

Much of this happens because Christians do not understand the concept of worship. They often relegate it to a structured period of time: "Now we're going to have a worship service." Obviously, worship can and should take place during a "period of time," but meaningful worship can and should happen spontaneously throughout the time the church gathers to be built up in Christ. A heart that responds to the teaching of God's Word is worshiping. A heart that says "thank-you" to God when someone shares an answer to prayer is worshiping. A heart that says "I love You" to God when engaged in a moment of quiet meditation is also worshiping God. Worship happens whenever we "draw near to God," no matter what the circumstances or events. Worship should be interwoven with everything that happens when believers meet together. And when Christians are worshiping God, it can be sensed, felt, and observed. It is visible.

The second reflection of faith is *perseverance*—perseverance against sin. How frequently twentieth-century churches are plagued with bitterness, immorality, materialistic attitudes, and legalistic behavior. And how devastating these "weights" are in keeping Christians from reaching the goal of Christian maturity, of running the race well.

Yes, many twentieth-century churches have been calloused to sin. Church discipline is a forgotten biblical injunction. Few really seem to care, and ministers are often afraid to confront people with sin problems lest they "stop giving" or "leave the church." Some people are actually paralyzed by the fear of being rejected by those who are living in sin.

How tragic! This is not faith—it is fear! But the Bible says that "there is no fear in love." Rather, "perfect love drives out fear" (1 John 4:18). This kind of love causes believers to really care about others who are sinning, to approach them in love and in non-judgmental ways. We must remember that those who really love people stop them from hurting themselves, from hurting the body of Christ, and most of all, from hurting the Lord Jesus.

Finally, *works* also reflect faith. Many twentieth-century Christians cannot really identify with New Testament sharing and giving. Frequently those pioneers of faith gave out of poverty. They gave when they themselves desperately needed what they gave away!

Most twentieth-century Christians (myself included) need to evaluate their program of giving. To what extent are we really sharing our material possessions in proportion to the way God has blessed us? There is much we can learn from the Macedonian Christians about whom Paul said the following: "And now, brothers, we want you to know about the grace that God has given the Macedonian churches. Out of the most severe trial, their overflowing joy and their extreme poverty welled up in rich generosity. For I testify that they gave as much as they were able, and even beyond their ability. Entirely on their own, they urgently pleaded with us for the privilege of sharing in this service to the saints" (2 Cor. 8:1-4).

ACTION STEP

Following is a series of questions that will help you and your church evaluate the extent to which you are reflecting New Testament faith:

WORSHIP: To what extent do we express our faith in worship? Is our relationship with God vital, dynamic, and real? Can people "see" our relationship with God in the way we approach Him? When the church gathers to worship, is the structure such that people sense freedom in worship? Or is the service so structured that only that which is "planned" can happen? Is there even room for spontaneity and freedom for the Holy Spirit to work through members of the body to help the whole body worship?

PERSEVERANCE: How seriously do we take the reality of sin in our own lives personally and in the body of Christ? To what extent is loving church discipline being administered when people sin? To what extent do we as individuals take this responsibility upon ourselves?

WORKS: To what extent are we demonstrating faith by our works, particularly in sharing our material possessions to meet the needs of God's work? (No doubt, some people in your church are giving regularly and systematically and even sacrificially. But if your church is true to form, many are not. Maturity is reflected in our giving when every member of the body of Christ gets involved in sharing according to the way God has prospered him.)

FAMILY OR GROUP PROJECT

Most of the criteria for measuring the maturity level of a church can also be applied to the family or to small groups within the body of Christ. Using these reflections of faith as a measuring rod, evaluate your situation. For example, as a family, are you able to approach God freely and spontaneously? Are you dealing with sin? Are you as a family, sharing your material possessions with others? More specifically, are you teaching your children to give proportionately to the church from their own personal income? Remember: it is rather difficult to teach our children to do something we are not doing ourselves.

chapter 12
PRODUCING A MATURE CHURCH

The characteristic of a mature church in the New Testament is abundantly clear. The degree in which *faith*, *hope* and *love* were expressed in a local church was the criterion that appears again and again as a standard used by New Testament leaders, particularly the apostle Paul.

How are these virtues cultivated and developed? What must happen if a body of believers is to become mature—reflecting a dynamic faith, a steadfast hope, and a Christlike love?

Again the Bible gives us the answer. Along with the *product*, it gives us the *process!*

Though the process for developing maturity in a local church is illustrated throughout the New Testament, Luke's record of the spiritual and numerical growth of the church in Jerusalem brings all of the necessary ingredients of this process together in one succinct and classic paragraph—Acts 2:42-47.

VITAL LEARNING EXPERIENCES
WITH THE WORD OF GOD

Luke records that these New Testament believers in Jerusalem "devoted themselves to the apostles' teaching . . ." (Acts 2:42). This teaching, of course, included those New Testament doctrines that were given to the apostles by direct revelation from God. When Jesus ate the Last Supper with the twelve, He made a promise to the apostles, and the events recorded in Acts are no doubt the fulfillment of this promise: "The Counselor, the Holy Spirit, whom the Father will send in my name, will teach you all things and will remind you of everything I have said to you" (John 14:26).

God, in His divine plan, has made it possible for believers today, those of us living in the twentieth-century, to still devote ourselves "to the apostles' teaching." The New Testament Scriptures contain those doctrines, beautifully and realistically woven into a variety of letters and written reports, many of which were penned directly to New Testament churches to help them become mature in Christ. What a creative way to relate doctrine to life, rather than to give us a volume of systematic theology, all neatly outlined and arranged! Rather, God wants us to see doctrine in relationship to real-life experiences, and particularly in relationship to the problems we face as we live our Christian lives from day to day.

The apostles initiated the growth process in the believers' lives in Jerusalem by exposing them to Bible doctrine. And this process was also carefully followed by the apostle Paul and his fellow missionaries in their church-planting ministry. This is why Paul spent an entire year in Antioch teaching the disciples; a year and six months in Corinth; at least six months in Thessalonica; and a total of three years in Ephesus. This is why he even went beyond a personal ministry among new converts and often sent Timothy and others back to the churches to continue teaching these believers the basic doctrines of Christianity (1 Thess. 3:2; 1 Cor. 4:17; Titus 2:1). No church can develop maturity-reflecting faith, hope, and love without *vital learning experiences with the Word of God.*

VITAL RELATIONAL EXPERIENCES WITH EACH OTHER AND WITH GOD

Not only did these Jerusalem Christians devote themselves to "the apostles' teaching," but also "to the fellowship," that is, "the breaking of bread and to prayer. . . . They gave to anyone as he had need. . . . They broke bread in their homes and ate together with glad and sincere hearts, praising God and enjoying the favor of all the people" (Acts 2:42-47).

Luke records four relational-type experiences in this paragraph:

They Ate Together

"Breaking bread" in many New Testament churches was more than having communion once a month, using token elements—a morsel of bread and a sip of wine. Rather, they actually ate a meal together. On occasions, these meals were called "love feasts" (Jude 12; 2 Pet. 2:13). The Corinthians, of course, had to be severely admonished for misusing and abusing this meal (1 Cor. 11:17-34).

Love feasts were no doubt patterned after the Lord's Supper—the final meal which Jesus shared with His disciples before He faced the cross. During that meal, using the very elements they were eating and drinking together, Jesus broke bread and drank wine, admonishing

147

them to thereafter remember His broken body and shed blood.

The New Testament believers in Jerusalem took these instructions very seriously. In fact, it appears that most every time they had a meal together, as they went from house to house, they remembered the Lord's broken body and shed blood.

The important factor, of course, is not how often we remember the Lord in this way, or what kind of specific elements we use. Rather, the essence of this experience was fellowship—eating together and at the same time, remembering the death of the Lord Jesus Christ. Here we see a dramatic interrelationship between human relationships and a relationship with God. As they ate together (at the horizontal level) they also remembered the Lord together (at the vertical level)!

They Prayed Together

Prayer among New Testament believers was usually also in the context of human relationships. In other words, prayer frequently involved the body of Christ. It was a corporate experience.

Note the context of prayer in the following passages, the context indicating body relationships:

"Be devoted to one another in brotherly love. Honor one another above yourselves. Never be lacking in zeal, but keep your spiritual fervor, serving the Lord. Be joyful in hope, patient in affliction, *faithful in prayer.* Share with God's people who are in need. Practice hospitality" (Rom. 12:10-13).

"And we urge you, brothers, warn those who are idle, encourage the timid, help the weak, be patient with everyone. Make sure that nobody pays back wrong for wrong, but always try to be kind to each other and to everyone else. Be joyful always; *pray continually;* give thanks in all circumstances, for this is God's will for you in Christ Jesus" (1 Thess. 5:14-18).

"Is anyone of you in trouble? He should *pray.* Is anyone happy? Let him sing songs of praise. Is anyone of you sick? He should call the elders of the church to *pray* over him and anoint him with oil in the name of the Lord. And the prayer offered in faith will make the sick person well; the Lord will raise him up. If he has sinned, he will be forgiven. Therefore, confess your sins to each other and *pray for each other* so that you may be healed. The prayer of a righteous man is powerful and effective" (Jas. 5:13-16).

"The end of all things is near. Therefore be clear-minded and self-controlled so that you can *pray.* Above all, love each other deeply, because love covers over a multitude of sins. Offer hospitality to one another without grumbling. Each one should use whatever spiritual gift he has received to serve others, faithfully administering God's grace in its various forms" (1 Pet. 4:7-10).

Evidently, New Testament "prayer meetings" did not usually involve "periods of prayer" or a "time" or an "evening" or a "day" set aside for prayer, though on occasions this was done. Rather, the normal process involved prayer, interwoven into a variety of experiences, as believers met together to be edified. And most significantly, prayer at the vertical level was frequently prompted by needs at the horizontal level. Prayer was oriented around human relationships and needs, which gave it meaning and vitality at the divine level.

They Shared Their Material Possessions

In Jerusalem the believers actually launched a communal society, primarily because of persecution and because of human need that wasn't being met. They also, no doubt, thought that Christ was coming back immediately to deliver them from this world system.

The communal pattern, of course, is not the important issue in the New Testament. In fact, this structure in Jerusalem was soon replaced when persecution drove the Christians out of the city.

The important thing is that New Testament Christians were "sharing" Christians. Whenever there were physical needs, they did what they could to meet those needs. They shared their material possessions with each other.

Again we must note that "giving" among New Testament Christians was in the context of human relationships. And as they gave to meet each others' needs, they were remembering and honoring the Lord Jesus Christ, who gave everything for us that we might have life—the One who said, "As I have loved you, so you must love one another" (John 13:34).

They Praised God Together

New Testament Christians praised God in various ways, one being corporate singing. Thus Paul wrote to both the Ephesians and Colossians, and exhorted them to speak to one another with psalms and hymns and spiritual songs, to sing and make melody in their hearts to the Lord (Eph. 5:19; Col. 3:16).

Note again that praising God with song was so interrelated with human relationships that it cannot be functionally separated. As they spoke to one another, using musical expressions, they lifted their voices and hearts in praise and thanksgiving to God. Again, human relationships gave meaning to their relationship with God.

Thus we see that New Testament Christians had vital relationships with each other and with God. And these two relationships were significantly interrelated. As they ate their meals together, they remembered the Lord in holy communion; as they prayed for one another, they talked to God; as they gave their material possessions to meet each other's needs, they worshiped the One who gave His life for them; and as they taught one another with psalms and hymns and spiritual songs, they were lifting their voices in praise and thanksgiving to God!

VITAL WITNESSING EXPERIENCES WITH THE UNSAVED WORLD

The final statement in Luke's paragraph states that "the Lord added to their number daily those who were being saved." But this must not be interpreted out of context. These Christians were "enjoying the favor of all the people." Thus many non-Christians were very impressed with this new life-style, this new faith in Christ, this new and vibrant community of love. Consequently, many of them put their faith in Christ and joined themselves to this body of believers.

New Testament Christians were dynamic. They infected and affected the community in which they lived. And many people responded to their testimony and witness.

The most important ingredient that impressed these non-Christians was the community of love. This was the significant factor that communicated the reality of Christ to those who did not know Him. As they saw the believers in Jerusalem *eating* together, *praying* for one another, *sharing* their possessions with each other, and *praising* God, they held them in high regard. Their life-style, their love for one another, became the "bridge" that reached these people for Jesus Christ—the means which caused them to respond to the gospel. This was a dramatic fulfillment of Christ's statement: "All men will know that you are my disciples if you love one another" (John 13:35).

THE TWENTIETH-CENTURY CHURCH

To become a mature New Testament church in the twentieth century we must have the same three vital experiences as the New Testament church in the first century. We need not one, not two, but all three experiences—and in balance.

Some churches tend to focus on one of these experiences. Note what happens:

Churches that emphasize Bible teaching to the exclusion of fellowship and sharing Christ soon become *cold* and *academic.*

Churches that emphasize fellowship and neglect Bible teaching and sharing Christ soon become *superficial* and *emotional.*

Churches that emphasize evangelism and neglect Bible teaching and fellowship are filled with people *starved* for the Word of God and *hungry* for deep relationships.

Many churches tend to focus on two of these experiences. Note what happens to them:

Churches that emphasize Bible teaching and fellowship but neglect evangelism often become *ingrown* and *stagnant.* There is no fresh flow of new life that keeps a church vibrant and pulsating with New Testament dynamic.

Churches that emphasize fellowship and evangelism and neglect Bible teaching often get off into *false doctrine* and create splinter groups.

Churches that emphasize Bible teaching *and* evangelism but neglect relational Christianity produce Christians who know the Word and share it but never feel comfortable in developing deep relationships with other Christians—an absolute essential if we are to be mature New Testament Christians.

May I emphasize again, to become a mature New Testament church we must have all three of these experiences and in balance. We need not one, not two, but all three experiences.

We see, then, that our churches can often be categorized according to their emphases, and, consequently, their weaknesses.

There are the *Bible* churches. There are the *relational* churches. There are the big *evangelistic* churches. There are the ingrown churches—the Bible teaching and fellowship type churches, but without outreach. There are the fellowship and evangelistic type churches, but without a deep knowledge of the Word of God. There are the Bible teaching and evangelism churches, but without deep relationships.

But where are the churches that are striving for balance? Unfortunately, they seem to be few and far between. And if this balance does not exist, *faith, hope* and *love* will not emerge as the marks of maturity. Rather, we will discover ourselves evaluating our success by how many Bible meetings and seminars we offer; or on the basis of how much time we spend in small groups; or on the basis of how many people are being added to the church. All of these things *could* indicate maturity, but they are all *means* to an end! And if any one of these becomes an "end" in itself, faith, hope and love will not emerge as the distinguishing marks of a New Testament church.

ACTION STEP

One of the major problems facing twentieth-century

churches is making non-absolutes absolute. We have come to equate tradition with biblical truth. We have confused patterns and principles. We have allowed our forms and structures to dictate what we do, rather than the supra-cultural guidelines of the Bible.

One thing is certain. There is no absolute pattern for developing faith, hope and love in a church! God has left us free to develop the forms and structures that will help us to be a New Testament church in the twentieth-century—wherever we may be located. What may work in one community may not work in another. Thus, it is dangerous to borrow programs. What we must do is search out and apply the supra-cultural principles of the Bible—those principles that will work in any culture and at any given moment in history.

With this in mind, evaluate your church. The following questions will help you:

1. Do the forms and structures of my church allow for a balance in learning the Word of God, in having relational experiences with one another and with God, and in sharing Christ with others?

Unsatisfactory   1   2   3   4   5   Satisfactory

2. Is the Word of God taught clearly and regularly?

Unsatisfactory   1   2   3   4   5   Satisfactory

     a. Is the Word of God taught with variety—verse by verse, topical studies, biographical studies, etc., or are we "locked in" to one particular approach?

Unsatisfactory   1   2   3   4   5   Satisfactory

     b. Is there a good balance between teaching from the Old Testament and the New Testament?

Unsatisfactory   1   2   3   4   5   Satisfactory

c. Is the Word of God applied to twentieth-century life and practice?

Unsatisfactory   1   2   3   4   5   Satisfactory

d. Am I learning how to study the Word of God on my own?

Unsatisfactory   1   2   3   4   5   Satisfactory

3. Do our structures allow for relationships with God to grow naturally out of relationships with people?

Unsatisfactory   1   2   3   4   5   Satisfactory

a. Do our structures and approaches allow for communion to be a meaningful experience, involving deep relationships with people?

Unsatisfactory   1   2   3   4   5   Satisfactory

b. Is prayer vital and dynamic, based on an awareness of human needs in the body, or are we locked into traditional approaches to prayer that make it nonpersonal, nebulous, general, and meaningless?

Unsatisfactory   1   2   3   4   5   Satisfactory

c. Is giving spontaneous, regular, and joyful in the context of meeting the needs of people? Or is giving a mechanical process that we are expected to engage in, without knowing what the needs are for which we are giving or how the money is used?

Unsatisfactory   1   2   3   4   5   Satisfactory

d. Does our music represent a balance between songs and hymns that teach and admonish one another and those that exalt and glorify God? And do we have freedom to use music that is expressed in various ways, or do we lock ourselves in to music that we are culturally conditioned to accept and appreciate?

Unsatisfactory   1   2   3   4   5   Satisfactory

4. Do our structures allow opportunities to share Christ with others? Or are we so busy running to the church and attending meetings that we don't have time to share Christ—to build bridges with non-Christians?

Unsatisfactory   1   2   3   4   5   Satisfactory

5. Do we have time to relate to members of the body of Christ outside of the church building—in our homes, in recreational settings, and in the context of informality? Or do our relationships with people consist of attending meetings together, sitting in long rows, and listening to someone talk to us?

Unsatisfactory   1   2   3   4   5   Satisfactory

6. Do we have time to be with our families? Or do the church structures compete with our family life, allowing little time to be together?

Unsatisfactory   1   2   3   4   5   Satisfactory

7. Finally, do our church structures make us feel like we are on a "religious treadmill" running, running, running—and getting more tired with every passing week? (If so, something is wrong with our approach to church life. And chances are you will see little evidence of faith, hope, and love in the body of Christ—at least as these are defined in the New Testament.)

Unsatisfactory   1   2   3   4   5   Satisfactory

A FINAL WORD

Producing a mature church is an unusual challenge! If you are a pastor, remember that your greatest tool is the Bible. People who believe the Bible, can be reached *with* the Bible—providing its principles are used sensitively and in love.

The apostle Paul spoke to this issue when writing to Timothy: "Don't have anything to do with foolish and stupid arguments, because you know they produce quarrels. And the Lord's servant must not quarrel; instead, he must be kind to everyone, able to teach, not resentful. Those who oppose him he must gently instruct, in the hope that God will give them a change of heart leading them to a knowledge of the truth" (2 Tim. 2:23-25).

There is no doubt that many churches need to be renewed, that Christians need to be awakened to their tendency to serve the structures of the church rather than the divine purposes for which the church exists, and that they frequently use a false criteria for evaluating their functions. But there is no excuse for insensitivity, tactlessness and defensiveness in our attempts to renew the church. We must be on guard as we shepherd the flock of God, that we do not violate the very principles we believe in.

And finally, if you are not in a leadership role in your church, prayerfully share this book with those who are. Ask them to read it and give you their evaluation. Don't approach them as if it has all the answers—because it doesn't! Rather, you might say: "Here is a book reflecting the thinking of a pastor and professor who is exploring the Scriptures to discover God's standard for measuring the maturity level of a local church. If he's wrong at some point, he is open to your suggestions and corrections!"